STUDIES IN ENGLISH LITERATURE

Volume XXXI

NATURE REDEEMED

THE IMITATION OF ORDER
IN THREE RENAISSANCE POEMS

by

ERIC LAGUARDIA

University of Washington

1966

MOUTON & CO.

LONDON · THE HAGUE · PARIS

Printed in The Netherlands

TO KAY

CONTENTS

INTRODUCTION

This study of the representation of a redeemed natural world in three poems of the English Renaissance has its historical foundation in the effort of the age to formulate a conception of universal order which expressed a new awareness of the world of nature as well as the older belief in the supremacy of the City of God. The idea of order provoked by this shift in interest from the heavenly to the earthly consisted of an equitable relationship between the natural world and the divine world. According to this relationship the sensual demands made upon man by nature are not renounced in favor of a supernatural fulfillment of man in God; but the divine world is still thought of as the source of perfect order and goodness. The conception of universal order which developed in the Renaissance thus depends on a separation *and* a commerce between the natural and the divine. The two worlds are separate in the sense that a perfection of man and the civil and natural worlds around him is possible without transcending the human condition in favor of the divine condition. There is a commerce between the earthly and the heavenly in the sense that the perfection of the natural world can be accomplished only by bringing the content of the temporal world into accord with the content of the eternal world.

The natural world, of course, is thought to be in a fallen condition; the fall is a necessary preliminary to the restoration of the world to its rightful position as a replica of the perfect order of heaven. A significant aspect of this Renaissance conception of universal order is the belief that the natural world (including man) has the capacity for being redeemed or perfected. Nature and man may be in a fallen condition, but within them are unfulfilled forces of goodness and order. The process of releasing these forces results in a redeemed world, a world which has been brought back into alignment with the eternal order of the divine. Nature and man also have the capacity for corruption and damnation; within the world there is the potential danger of total imperfection. Thus, nature has a double characteristic: it may, both physically and morally, become permanently corrupt, or it may be restored to its proper condition as a temporal counterpart to the eternal order. The objective of a perfected natural order is reached by rejecting and removing the perverse forces within nature and releasing the forces of goodness and order inherent in the world. The resulting condition of concord and harmony is one in which nature is cleansed of its moral and physical corruptions, but not one in which nature is renounced completely in favor of the redemption of man in the heavenly city.

In Renaissance poetry, this conception of a perfected or redeemed natural world is the source of a number of themes concerned with the conflict within nature between the corrupting and the purifying, a conflict ultimately resolved by the restoration of order and goodness to the world. This general thematic interest gives meaning to the three poems of Spenser, Milton, and Shakespeare examined in the following pages. In addition, it is maintained that all of these writers create a fictional world which corresponds structurally to the characteristics of the picture of world order outlined above. The Renaissance conception of universal harmony which consists of the suppression of what is demonic and the release of what is divine in nature is translated into poetry through a thematic interest in the perfecting or redeeming of the world. In addition, the form given to this theme reproduces a natural world which is both demonic and divine. The emphasis in this study is not upon the intellectual history of the Renaissance ideal of a perfect world. It is, rather, upon artistically imitated worlds which reveal in their themes and forms the Renaissance concern with the problem of making nature resemble the divine order without letting the heavenly take the place of the earthly.

Books III and IV of *The Faerie Queene, Comus,* and *All's Well That Ends Well* all have as a poetic objective the establishment of an integrated and ordered natural world. The objective is reached only after the conflict within nature between the perverse and the pure is resolved. The objective, in addition, consists of that particular kind of equitable relationship between the natural and the divine which requires a bond between the two realms but not an exact equation of nature and spirit. The Renaissance effort to find a place in the order of things for the forces and drives of life but yet not to give up that ideal of a world divinely arranged by the mind of God is responsible for this careful balance between the temporal demands of nature and the immanence of the divine in the world. In these three poems, the resolution of the conflict between what nature demands of man sensually and what the divine world permits him to do rationally is imaginatively achieved by representing the progress of man and nature toward a condition which is animated both morally and physically by the order and purity of the divine. It is a solution which allows man to be redeemed within nature, but within a nature which has been cleansed of its perverting, imbruting, and lustful aspects. The conclusion of all these poems is, in other words, a perfection or redemption of the natural world rather than a transcendence of nature. The poetic world which prevails finally is informed by the divine but not replaced by it.

In addition to having similar poetic objectives, all of the poems express conflict and resolution in similar terms. The opposition between the libertine and the chaste heroine appears in each poem, and, in various forms, this clash of sensuality and purity is resolved in the concord of chaste love. It is maintained that the strife in these poems between lawless sensuality and virginal purity is a figurative way of indicating the larger opposition in the world between total earthly corruption and total earthly purity. In the attempt to create imaginatively a world harmony consistent with the ideals of the age, the choice of either *total* corruption or *total* purity would be unsatisfactory. To submit to the totally corrupt level of nature would, of course, destroy the world's potential for perfection. To submit to the totally pure would also prevent the perfection of nature, for nature cannot be fulfilled unless sexual passion is allowed its place. The compromise or the balance between lawless sensuality and virginal purity is expressed in these poems through chaste love. It is clear that this kind of solution avoids the negative aspects of both extremes, and serves as a new and single reality. Love is accepted in nature by this compromise, but it is a love purged of any wanton desire by the power of chastity. It is further maintained that chaste love, by virtue of its ability to reconcile the two extremes of the natural world in a sensuous but virtuous condition, serves in these poems as a figure for a perfected or redeemed world.

A poetic theme which depends on a view of nature aligned with the divine rather than of nature transcended by the divine requires a poetic structure made up of an action which takes place in nature but which may have divine meaning, a setting which is natural but which may have divine characteristics, and imagery which is capable of expressing the bond between the earthly and the heavenly. The fictional worlds of these three poems have their roots in the natural world, but the influence of the divine is apparent. In addition to representing the heavenly in the earthly, these poems also represent the hellish in the earthly, for nature has a potential for damnation as well as salvation. The eternal worlds of heaven and hell are not literally identified in these fictional worlds, but their agents are everywhere evident, and their effect on nature is made clear. Thus, the imitated worlds of these three poems correspond both thematically and structurally to the ideal of world order projected by a pervasive tradition in Renaissance culture.

The first two chapters are devoted to putting down some foundations necessary for the application of my argument in the final chapters on the poems themselves. Chapter One deals with Renaissance views concerning the double aspect of nature, part demonic and part divine. It also deals with a Renaissance conception of the potential of man in a world divided between God and the devil. And finally the first chapter deals with the conflict between passion and purity, or between Venus and Diana. The intention in the three sections of this chapter is to move steadily away from the large polarity between a demonic and divine nature in the direction of the smaller but highly metaphorical polarity of passion and purity.

Chapter Two is devoted to a discussion of relevant aspects of the theories of the imitation of nature. The intention is that some of the characteristics of the mode of imitation in Renaissance poetry should be clarified before looking directly at the texts of the three poems. The first section of this chapter deals with Erich Auerbach's distinction between the figural and the secular representation of reality in literature, with the intention of borrowing historical and critical support for the central observation that the imitation of reality in the three Renaissance poems is restricted to nature, yet expresses the link between nature and hell and nature and heaven. The second section is concerned with relevant aspects of the Renaissance ideas of poetic imitation and decorum, with the intention of providing a theoretical and historical basis for the claim that the three poems of Spenser, Milton, and Shakespeare imitate a "perfected" nature. And, finally, in the third section Northrop Frye's conception of the "romantic" mode of imitation is considered in order to provide an organized approach to the critical examination of the Renaissance poems in the last chapters.

There is evidence in the Renaissance of a shift away from an interest in a transcendent order of perfection toward a belief in a divinely arranged order of nature as sufficient ground for the fulfillment of man and nature. These three Renaissance works have been chosen in order to demonstrate that this shift from the heavenly to the earthly is an organic part of the theme and structure of representative English Renaissance poetry. In each of the poems metaphorical techniques are employed with great brilliance to reveal the immanence of spirit (and demon) in the world of nature. The goal of this form of expression is the imitation of a natural world restored to its proper location just below the eternal perfection of the divine world. It is an imitation which includes in its vision of reality the passionate demands of the natural in harmonious conjunction with the ideal of purity.

I have been attracted by the beauty and the effectiveness of

these works, if not always by their success in completing a
dramatic intention. But my primary intention in this study is not
to evaluate the excellence of the poetry by any appeal to touch-
stones of greatness. I want, rather, to make a tacit appeal for
their relevance, both thematically and structurally, to that remarkable ability of the English Renaissance imagination to con-
vert to poetry the vision of a world animated by the impulse of
passion as well as by the requirements of a constructive ethical
force.

I. NATURE AND SPIRIT

A. THE DOUBLE LAW OF NATURE

Fulke Greville, at the end of *Mustapha*, plaintively inquires: "what meaneth nature by these diverse laws?" Such a question is symptomatic of that concern of the Renaissance with the relationship between the worlds of nature and spirit, and the effort, both doctrinal and poetic, to come to some conclusion about their continuity or discontinuity. To consider nature in a double aspect, as did Greville and many of his contemporaries, meant that it was seen to be, like Spenser's personification, both ugly and beautiful, and that it made both evil and virtuous demands upon man. In this widespread and familiar tradition of Renaissance thought, the diversity of nature's laws pointed in two directions: toward the beautiful, the harmonious, the virtuous, and ultimately to the eternal order of the world of spirit; or toward the ugly, the chaotic, the sinful, and ultimately to the eternal disorder of hell. The supernatural surrounds nature, the divine influencing it from above and the demonic from below. The primary concern of this tradition is, however, with the world of nature itself, and those aspects of it which form links between it and the supernatural worlds of hell and heaven. Although these two eternal realms establish the extremes of the opposition of disorder and order, it is the function of the demonic and the divine *within nature* with which the thought of this tradition is most concerned.

A number of conflicts is characteristic of this double view of nature. That law which links nature with the world of spirit is rational; the content of that other aspect of nature, which can hardly be said to be governed by law, is irrational. The rational law can illuminate the world with true love; the irrational darkens the world with lust. One dimension of nature is invoked by metaphors of serenity, musical harmony, purity, and reconciliation; the other by metaphors of tempests, discords, foulness, and separation. Angelic man is the result of a victory for one side of nature; brutish man of a victory for the other side. Nature, in short, may be either in accord with the world of spirit or opposed to it. If it is in accord with the world of spirit, it is physically ordered and morally acceptable. If it is not, it is disordered and morally corrupting.

Richard Hooker has given form to that law of nature which reveals the commerce between the natural and the divine:

That law, the performance whereof we behold in things natural, is as it were an authentical or an original draught written in the bosom of God himself; whose Spirit being to execute the same useth every particular nature, every mere natural agent, only as an instrument created at the beginning, and ever since the beginning used, to work his own will and pleasure withal. Nature therefore is nothing else but God's instrument.[1]

The law of which Hooker speaks is natural and eternal; nature is a function of spirit and reflects its absolute laws.[2] The term "law of nature" or "natural law" is employed by Hooker to indicate that there is a continuity between nature and spirit (and will be so employed in the discussion here). In the tradition of thought with which I am concerned, the other dimension of nature can only be said to have a "law" in the ironic sense, as in Comus' accusation that the Lady has betrayed the covenants of nature's trust, and thus those forces which control this aspect of nature will not be referred to here as "law". Those forces can, however,

---

[1] *Of the Laws of Ecclesiastical Polity* (Everyman's Library, London, 1907), I, 160.
[2] Described by William Ames in *Conscience With the Power and Cases Thereof* (1639): "The right natural, or natural law, is the same which usually is called the eternal law. But it is called eternal in relation to God, as it is from eternity in him. It is called natural as it is engrafted and imprinted in the nature of man by the God of nature." Quoted from A. S. P. Woodhouse, ed., *Puritanism and Liberty* (Chicago, 1951), p. 187.

be spoken of as functions of the eternal world of the demonic in nature, just as the "law of nature" expresses the function of the eternal world of the divine in nature.

For Hooker, since the law of nature has its origin in the *lex aeterna*, the maintenance of total cosmic harmony depends upon man's obedience of that law of nature:

Now if nature should intermit her course, and leave altogether though it were but for a while the observation of her own laws; if those principal and mother elements of the world, whereof all things in this lower world are made, should lose the qualities which now they have; if the frame of that heavenly arch erected over our heads should loosen and dissolve itself; if celestial spheres should forget their wonted motions, and by irregular volubility turn themselves any way as it might happen; if the prince of the lights of heaven, which now as a giant doth run his wearied course, should as it were through a languishing faintness begin to stand and to rest himself; if the moon should wander from her beaten way, the times and seasons of the year blend themselves by disordered and confused mixture, the winds breathe out their last gasp, the clouds yield no rain, the earth be defeated of heavenly influence, the fruits of the earth pine away as children at the withered breasts of their mother no longer able to yield them relief: what would become of man himself, whom these things now all do serve? See we not plainly that obedience of creatures unto the law of nature is the stay of the whole world? [3]

The same order which maintains the proper functioning of the elemental world and allows the cycle of nature to complete itself, requires a moral conduct in man which is similarly reasonable and harmonious. The image which Hooker sketches is of a perfected nature. It is a world which is distinct from, but intimately aligned with the realm of spirit. It is implicit in the passage above, and explicit throughout the *Laws*, that the perfected natural world is a nature which responds both elementally and morally to the original pattern of order and purity of the supernatural world of the divine.

This formidable correspondence which was said to bind the natural to the divine world was, unfortunately, only an immense ideal. In spite of the belief in the intimate correspondence between the microcosm and the macrocosm, and the affirmations

[3] *Laws,* I, 157.

of the existence of this relationship, it was recognized that man did not obey the law of nature. As a result the entire natural world was viewed as corrupt. Richard Cavendish, in *The Image of Nature and Grace*, describes the origin of this disobedience and corruption with obvious relish:

Here entred our first soyle and haynous infection, namely our originall sinne, the deprivation and ruine of whole nature, the spoyle and corruption of all vertues, both of body and mynde, the swallowing sea of all confusion, the cursed cloud of ignorance, the deepe darkener of all devine knowledge: the ruinous roote of all outrage, the mother of all contempt, the hed and fountayne of all synne: the banysher of reason, and surrenderer of all the raynes, and government of lyfe into the handes of licentious lusts, and filthy affections.[4]

Athough the perfect order and goodness of nature was said to be destroyed, the ideal of natural law was not. Man and nature had fallen, but regeneration, the realignment of the natural and the spiritual, was still possible. Such a restoration served as a goal rather than a reality; and especially as a goal of poetry, in which the ideal of a nature redeemed of its corruptions and realigned with the content of the divine world could be vividly expressed. As a poetic theme, this desire to declare the existence of a continuity between the natural and the supernatural takes the significant form of the restoration of nature itself and man within nature. This Renaissance tradition of thought and expression which can, in general, be identified by its concern over the breach between the order of nature and the order of spirit, and by its effort to affirm some kind of reconciliation of the two orders, is less interested in the salvation of man in a realm beyond nature than it is in the restoration of man within nature and the redemption of the natural world itself. Such an interest requires that nature be properly used rather than transcended, for the emphasis remains upon nature even though its restoration consists of releasing those forces which link it with the world of spirit.

Because of this new emphasis in the Renaissance on the world of nature, it was not only necessary to establish the reality of that upper dimension of nature which revealed the influence of the divine world, but also to remove those corrupting aspects of

[4] (London, 1571), pp. 7a-b.

the lower dimension of nature which revealed the influence of the eternally demonic world. The removal of those aspects, however, amounts to a purification rather than a complete rejection of the lower dimension of nature, for this level of the natural world is identified with the forces of life, its instincts and passions. To reject this dimension of nature would be to reject nature itself. The problem is, then, how to maintain the bond between the natural world and the virtuous order of the divine world without submitting to the corruptions of the sensual dimension of nature, but also without totally renouncing the value of sensual experience. The solution, of course, is that the two diverse dimensions of nature – which may be called here the sensual and the rational – must reach some kind of balance, a harmony which neither removes man from nature and places him in the realm of eternal purity, nor allows men wholly to submit to sensual disorder. This reconciliation constitutes the restoration of fallen man within nature. It is a reconciliation of the double and contradictory aspects of nature which brings the entire natural world back into alignment or continuity with the world of the divine. And it is in the poetry of the period that this ideal vision of the age is most vividly expressed. It takes the form not only of the restoration of man within nature, but also of the purification or redemption of the whole of nature. It is this image of a perfected nature, both elementally and morally, which is the objective of the three poems of Spenser, Shakespeare, and Milton to be examined below.

There are traditions of thought in the age running against the tradition with which I am here concerned. Hiram Haydn, in *The Counter-Renaissance*, indicates a fundamental distinction between some of these traditions:

... where the Scholastics and Christian humanists bent all their efforts toward an effectual wedding of reason and faith, reason and nature, theory and fact, the ideal and the actual, the hypothetical and the empirical – these heretics of the Counter-Renaissance wrought mightily to achieve their *separation*. And always their efforts were in the interest of depreciating the speculative intellect and the guidance of right reason. They variously place almost exclusive value in faith, in natural instinct, in "fact," in the empirically actual ....[5]

[5]   (New York, 1950), p. xv.

In both the humanistic tradition (with which I am concerned) and the tradition of the Counter-Renaissance, the content of the world of nature is distinguished from the content of the world of spirit. But in the more orthodox tradition, although the ideal of a nature perfected through "natural law" is cherished as an objective, the actual condition of nature is viewed as fallen and thus its values are not to be used as a guide to conduct; while in the more rebellious tradition of the Counter-Renaissance in which the emphasis falls on actual experience and natural instinct, the values of the world of nature are not viewed as impure and thus are allowable as a guide to conduct. For the orthodox tradition, nature has two dimensions, of which only that ideal one linked to the values of the world of spirit provides the proper objective for fallen man and nature. The other dimension of nature is to be purged of its uncontrolled and corrupting sensuality, and its purified (not extinguished) values are then included in the vision of a perfected nature. The total objective is expressed in poetry as a condition of nature in which purity, reason, and passion are harmonized. While the aim of the orthodox tradition is, in general, to construct out of a two-dimensional nature the harmonious ideal of a one-dimensional nature, the more rebellious tradition began with a one-dimensional natural world and accepted the sufficiency of that world.[6]

It is of course the orthodox tradition which forms the intellectual background for the poetic creation of a redeemed nature, for nature must be seen as corrupted before it can be purified. In the poetry of this tradition, however, some of the attitudes of the Counter-Renaissance are included, primarily to serve as a foil for the ultimate expression of a perfected nature. In the poetry which deals with the conflicts of love, these attitudes appear in the form of what is usually called "libertine naturalism", or simply "naturalism". It is the attitude of Spenser's Acrasia, Shakespeare's Parolles, and Milton's Comus, who all, generally

---

[6]   See A. O. Lovejoy and George Boas, *Primitivism and Related Ideas in Antiquity* (Baltimore, 1935), pp. 252-3, 281-2, 447-56; and H. S. Wilson, "Some Meanings of 'Nature' in Renaissance Literary Theory", *Journal of the History of Ideas,* II (1941), 430-48.

speaking, advocate the wanton seizure of pleasure and beauty in order to fulfill the bounty of nature before it withers and dies. The content of the world of nature is totally sufficient for them; no influence from the world of spirit is allowed, or even recognized. When figures such as these appear within the dramatic context of a work which is devoted to the ultimate establishment of a nature aligned with spirit, it is of course impossible that they should be permitted to maintain the "pureness" of their position. They are, as it is to be expected, made to recognize the power of the divine world functioning in nature, proven to be evil, and finally purged from the scene. The tension which exists, in poetry of this kind, between the value of "naturalism" and the values represented by the concept of "natural law", provides the general terms for the conflict between those forces which would disorder nature and imbrute man, and those forces which work to raise a fallen nature to a level where its content is aligned but not identified with the world of spirit. In conflict are two views of experience: nature may contain her own "laws" not only distinct from, but totally unrelated to the world of spirit; or nature may be "nothing else but God's instrument".[7]

The dramatic tension in poetry between naturalism and natural law reflects the larger issue of the relationship (separation or interaction) between nature and spirit, for the victory of natural law over naturalism is an affirmation of the functioning of the divine world in the natural, a declaration of the interaction of nature and spirit. This emphasis on nature, in the sense that the desired objective is the alignment with rather than the absorption by the world of spirit, reveals a significant aspect of much poetic representation of reality in the Renaissance. There are two basic

[7] For a more complete discussion of these two views of nature see: Louis I. Bredvold, "The Naturalism of Donne in Relation to Some Renaissance Traditions", *Journal of English and Germanic Philology*, XXII (1923), pp. 471-502; John F. Danby, *Shakespeare's Doctrine of Nature* (London, 1949), pp. 20-43; Theodore Spencer, *Shakespeare and the Nature of Man* (New York, 1942), pp. 1-50; Herschel Baker, *The Wars of Truth* (Cambridge, Mass., 1952); Geoffrey Bush, *Shakespeare and the Natural Condition* (Cambridge, Mass., 1956), pp. 3-19; Marjorie Hope Nicolson, *The Breaking of the Circle* (Evanston, Ill., 1950); and E. M. W. Tillyard, *The Elizabethan World Picture* (New York, 1944).

answers to the problem raised by a concern with the relationship between nature and spirit. One answer is a conception of reality in which the natural world is completely renounced in favor of the sufficiency of the world of spirit, or at least is thought to be at best an important preliminary stage in the process of man's redemption in the heavenly world. The other answer develops from the two-fold conception of nature, according to which the higher level of nature (carrying the stamp of the world of spirit) exerts its influence on the lower level of nature. The final effect of this action is the reconciliation of the demands of the flesh and the reason, which brings the world of nature into a closer relationship with the world of spirit, without, however, surrendering those qualities which characterize it as natural. In the first instance the objective is, in the words of Pico, to "disdain earthly things, strive for heavenly things, and finally, esteeming less whatever is of the world, hasten to that court which is beyond the world and nearest to the Godhead".[8] Such a goal indicates that nature is not to be redeemed, but removed as a barrier between man and spirit. In the second instance the objective is the redemption rather than the renunciation of the natural world, for those forces which account for the gross impurity of nature are meant to be purified and brought into accord with the world of spirit. For such a conception of reality the relationship between nature and spirit must be composed of a subtle balance in which the natural is not transcended by the supernatural, or is the influence of the supernatural totally removed from the natural.

In poetry the problem of constructing a relationship between nature and spirit which expresses the vision of a redeemed world is a problem of the imagination rather than of theology. The great image of a perfected elemental and human nature provoked and stimulated much of the humanistic thought of the age, but only in art does this image take form. Available to the poets was that four-fold conception of the cosmos which divided the universe into four levels of "existence". The different levels may be

---

[8] "Of the Dignity of Man", trans. Elizabeth L. Forbes, *Journal of the History of Ideas,* III (1942), 350.

summarized as follows: (1) The world of spirit, or the eternal world of the divine, the content of which is the source of all purity and order; the *lex aeterna*. (2) The highest level of nature; its "law of nature" reveals the workings of the *lex aeterna* in the natural world. (3) The lowest level of nature, characterized by lust and corruption; it reveals the presence of Satan in nature. (4) The eternal world of hell and the demonic. In the poetry of Spenser, Shakespeare, and Milton to be discussed below, this four-fold universe provides a fundamental structure for the imitation of a perfected nature and the conflict which precedes that restoration. The process begins with the conflict in the fallen world between elements of (2) and (3). The resolution consists of the removal of the influence of (3), but not with a rejection of the generative and sensual aspects of nature. Such a conclusion provides an image of a redeemed natural world in that both the values of spirit and nature are harmonized.

B. THE POTENTIAL OF MAN

It is necessary to elaborate somewhat on the second and third parts of the above scheme, for the necessity of and the possibility for a redemption of nature depends on the conflict in the fallen world between those forces associated with the eternal worlds of (1) and (4). The goal of perfected nature implies not only a fallen world, but also the potential of that world to become purified. This potential of course is suggested by (2) and (3) in the scheme; either one of the sets of values may claim the allegiance of man. There are two forms which the physical world also may take:

> Whoso hath seen, how one warm lump of wax
> (Without increasing, or decreasing) takes
> A hundred figures; well may judge of all
> Th' incessant Changes of this neather Ball.
> The Worlds owne Matter is the waxen Lump,
> Which, un-self-changing, takes all kind of stamp:
> The Form's the Seal; Heav'ns gratious Emperour
> (The living God) 's the great *Lord Chancellour*;

> Who at his pleasure setting day and night
> His great *Broad Seales*, and *Privy Signets* right
> Upon the Mass so vast and variable,
> Makes the same Lump, now base, now honourable.[9]

These variations are limited to the world of matter itself. But it is possible to view the natural world as not worthy of any attempt to make it "honourable":

> Now as the Wars prove man's mortality;
> So do the oppositions here below,
> Of Elements, the contrariety,
> Of constellations, which above do shew,
> Of qualities in flesh, will in the spirits;
> Principles of discord, not of concord made,
> All prove God meant not Man should here inherit
> A time-made World, which with time should not fade;
> But as Noah's flood once drowned woods, hills, & plain,
> So should the fire of Christ waste all again.[10]

Although the elemental aspect of nature may be redeemed of its corruptions, it is man, of course, on whom the theme of redemption centers; the restoration of himself, others, or the society around him is accompanied by a symbolic redemption of all nature. In the familiar Renaissance analogical view of the universe, man is thought to be an imperfect image of the macrocosm. Just as that range of the natural world below the sphere of the moon imperfectly represents the order of the higher spheres, man is corrupt when compared to the content of the eternal world above him. In spite of this corruption, man has another dimension; he is a *compositum mixtum*, linked not only to the corrupt level of nature, but also to the purity of the world of spirit.[11]

---

[9] Guillaume Du Bartas, *Divine Weeks,* trans. Joshua Sylvester (London, 1621), p. 23.

[10] Fulke Greville, *A Treatise of Wars, Poems and Dramas,* ed. Geoffrey Bullough (Edinburgh, 1938), Vol. I, p. 225.

[11] See Haydn, *The Counter-Renaissance,* p. 24: "The traditional Christian-humanist evaluation of man reminds us that his nature partakes of both the divine and the animal. With a love of analogy inherited from medieval thought, the Elizabethan describes again and again how the soul of man is compounded of all the ranks of the graded hierarchy of the creation. Yet man was most himself, the favorite child of the creation, when the rational part of his soul guided and controlled the lower parts, composed

Ralegh, in his *History of the World,* sees man as the bond between the angelic and brutal; the motion of his life "is always either increasing towards ripeness and perfection, or declining and decreasing towards rottenness and dissolution":

And whereas God created three sorts of living natures, (to wit) Angelical, Rational, and Brutal; giving to Angels an intellectual, and to Beasts a sensitive nature, he vouchsafed unto Man, both the intellectual of Angels, the sensitive of Beasts, and the proper rational belonging unto Man; and therefore . . . Man is the bond and chain which tieth together both Natures.[12]

In the translation of Gello's *Circe,* which was available in England in 1557, the same concept is expressed:

. . . Man is made of two natures, the one corporall and earthye, and the other heavenly and devyne: with the one of which he is lyke to brute beastes, and with the other to those immateriall substaunces that turne the heavens.[13]

The most effective presentation of this doctrine of man as *compositum mixtum* occurs in Bacon's allegorization of the myth of Pan, or nature, in *De dignitate et augmentis scientiarum.* Although Bacon's interpretation is primarily meant to represent the world of nature in the figure of bi-form Pan, his concept of nature includes man, and therefore man himself is bi-form in the same way:

The body of nature is likewise most aptly described as biform on account of the difference between bodies of the upper and lower world, whereof the former, from their beauty and regularity and constancy of motion as well as their influence over the Earth and earthly things, are properly represented by the human figure, human nature participating of order and dominion. But the latter, by reason of their perturbation and irregular movements, and because they are for the

---

of the passions and the appetites. Despite the contrary verdict of Luther and Calvin, the main line of Christian-humanism upheld the view that man, redeemed by Christ, was not hopelessly damned by original sin, and could find his own way to righteousness."

[12] (London, 1671), p. 23. First published, 1614.

[13] *Circes of John Baptista Gello,* trans. Henry Iden (London, 1557), Seventh Dialogue.

most part ruled by the heavenly bodies, may be content with the figure of a brute beast. Moreover this same description of a biform body has reference to the participation of species, for there is no natural species which can be regarded as simple, every one seeming to participate and be made up of two. Thus man has somewhat of the brute, the brute somewhat of the plant, the plant somewhat of the body inanimate, so that all things are indeed biform, being compounded of a superior and inferior species.[14]

The origin of Pan, according to Bacon, is threefold. He is the "offspring of the *Divine World*, through the medium of *confused matter* . . . and with the help of *Sin*, and by Sin Corruption entering in".[15] The brutish part of the figure of Pan is compensated

[14]   *Essays, Advancement of Learning, New Atlantis, and Other Pieces,* ed. R. F. Jones (New York, Odyssey Press, 1937), p. 399.

[15]   *Ibid.,* p. 397. That Pan or nature is the product of both the divine and the sinful is of course important to the conception of universal order being developed here. One view of nature maintained that the world is totally corrupt and demonic; another view maintained that nature possessed both demonic elements and divine possibilities. This latter view is the one which organizes the poetic theme of the redemption of nature. C. W. Lemmi, in *The Classical Deities in Bacon* (Baltimore, 1933), p. 74, comments on Bacon's three-fold interpretation as follows: "The interpretation is predominantly a Christian one; yet, as far as I know, the doctrine that God achieved the creation with the help of sin has not been advanced by any Christian theologian. Saint Augustine and Thomas Aquinas may be said to imply some such idea, for both regard sin as necessary to the harmonious completeness of God's work; but both are obviously indebted to the *Timaeus,* and it is Plato's God who deliberately creates mortal and corruptible beings with the help of a cooperating agency." The concept of nature as a combination of matter and divinity is evident in the two influential 12th century allegories, *De universitate mundi* of Bernard Silvestris, and *The Complaint of Nature* of Alain de Lille. Bernard's personification, Natura, accomplishes the formal organization of matter, which had been longing for order. To complete the creation man is made, but only with the help of divine and natural graces (Urania and Physis) so that he will be both angelic and human. The generative organs are praised as a restorer of nature and a preventer of the return of chaos. According to E. R. Curtius, Bernard gives us a sycretistic and essentially pagan picture of the universe. Natura "shares in the being of Godhead, but she is also linked to matter". Alain conceives of Natura as a goddess who "guiding the universe with thy reins, dost join all things in firmness with the knot of concord, and dost with the bond of peace marry heaven to earth" (trans. D. M. Moffat, *Yale Studies in English,* XXXVI [1908], 32-3). This concord has been destroyed by the victory of sense over reason in man, yet the laws of Natura, which bind nature to spirit, continue to exist and must be obeyed by man. See Curtius,

by his horns, a pyramidal form which reaches "even to the heaven . . . so easy and near a passage is it from the top of the pyramid to matters divine".[16]

This particular nature of man by which he may enjoy inter-course with both the sensual and the pure is not, however, an easy ambivalence. The conflict which it produces is pointed out by Justus Lipsius, the Belgian "high priest of Neostoicism" in the 16th century:

> . . . man consisteth of two parts, Soule and Body. That being the nobler part, resembleth the nature of a spirit and fire: This more base is compared to the earth. These two are joyned together, but yet with a jarring concord, as I may say, neither doe they easily agree, espe-cially when controversie ariseth about soverainty and subjection. For either of them would bear sway, and chiefly that part which ought not. The earth advanceth it selfe above the fire, and the dirty nature above that which is divine. Herehence arise in man dissentions, stirs, & a continual conflict of these parts warring together.[17]

And one of the most famous expressions of this conflict for man and the choices which lie before him is to be found in Pico's

---

European Literature and the Latin Middle Ages (New York, 1953), pp. 106-27; and E. C. Knowlton, "The Goddess Nature in Early Periods", *Journal of English and Germanic Philology*, XIX (1920), 224-53. Theodore Silverstein disagrees with Curtius that Bernard's work has a strong pagan coloring: "The Fabulous Cosmogony of Bernardus Silvestris", *Modern Philology*, XLVI (1948-9), 92-116.

[16] *Ibid.*, p. 398. The horns of Pan, reaching up to and providing passage to the divine world, exemplifies an important metaphorical tradition in the expression of the interaction between nature and spirit. It has its parallel in the concept of the sphere of the moon dividing the natural and the celestial worlds. The moon "separates the pure ether from the troubled atmosphere of the earth. It is the midpoint of the Golden Chain, navel of the upper and lower worlds" (Curtius, p. 111). Also relevant to this meta-phor are the doctrines of macrocosm-microcosm and *composition mixtum,* for both argue that man exists in a mediate position between spirit and sense: see Christopher Dawson, *Progress and Religion* (London, 1933), pp. 174-5. Examples of the metaphor of the midpoint between earth and heaven include the Earthly Paradise at the peak of the Mount of Purga-tory in the *Commedia*; and in Spenser: Arlo Hill, *The Faerie Queene,* 7.6-7, and the Temple of Venus, 4.10. Northrop Frye's term to describe this merger of the human and the divine is "epiphany": see *Anatomy of Criticism* (Princeton, 1957), pp. 203-6.

[17] *Two Bookes of Constancie,* ed. Rudolf Kirk (New Brunswick, N. J., 1939), p. 80.

oration "Of the Dignity of Man". In the imagined words of God:

> I have set thee at the world's center, that thou mayest from thence more easily observe whatever is in the world. I have made thee neither of heaven nor of earth, neither mortal nor immortal, so that thou mayest with greater freedom of choice and with more honor, as though the maker and moulder of thyself, fashion thyself in whatever shape thou shalt prefer. Thou shalt have the power to degenerate into the lower forms of life, which are animal; thou shalt have the power, out of thy soul's judgement, to be reborn into the higher forms of life, which are divine.[18]

Man, then, like nature, is a double creation with a potential for moving in either of two directions, depending on whether he employs his reason in order to align himself with the world of spirit, or whether he allows his brutish elements to drag him down. In poetry this conflict creates what Theodore Spencer calls the "dramatic tension of responsibility". It is man's responsibility, in the Christian conception of the progress of human history, to see that he plays "a conscious and rational part in the marvelous structure which the divine architect had created for him, so that he could praise the God who made him".[19]

It is appropriate now to narrow the discussion to the conflict of sense and reason, for these two capacities of man provide the terms by which the desired relationship between the spiritual and the natural may be expressed. The capacity of reason links man with the world of spirit; the capacity of sensuality distinguishes him from that world. The balancing of the two capacities, a reconciliation with the emphasis on the control of the sensual by the reason, provides a foundation in poetry for the imitation of a perfected natural world. This theme of reason-sensuality conflict is evident everywhere in the writings of the age. For Du Bartas it is a body-soul opposition:

[18] *Journal of the History of Ideas,* III (1942), 348.
[19] *Shakespeare and the Nature of Man,* p. 216. For additional statements of the doctrine of man as *compositum mixtum,* see: George Sandys, *Ovid's Metamorphosis Englished and Mythologized* (Oxford, 1632), p. 484; and Sir Thomas Browne, *Religio Medici* (London, Everyman's Library, 1951), p. 39.

> This rebell Flesh, whose counterpoize opresses
> My pilgrim Soule, and ever it depresses.[20]

For Davies the effect of the conflict is to make man both proud and wretched:

> I know my soule hath power to know all things,
> Yet is she blinde and ignorant in all;
> I know I am one of nature's little kings,
> Yet to the least and vilest things am thrall.
> I know my life's a paine and but a span,
> I know my Sense is mockt with every thing:
> And to conclude, I know my selfe a MAN,
> Which is a proud, and yet a wretched thing.[21]

Pleasure is a destructive force, as Sandys indicates in his allegorization of the Sirens in Ovid: ". . . the Sirens are now taken for inticing pleasures . . . and their musick for that eloquence which perswades to destruction".[22] And Chapman expresses the doctrine that bi-form man can only fulfill his angelic potential by moving away from pleasure:

> And that minde most is bewtifull and hye,
> And nearest comes to a Divinitie,
> That furthest is from spot of earths delight,
> Pleasures that lose their substance with their sight.[23]

It is the purification of sensual pleasure, however, rather than the total rejection of it which is important in the discussion here of a Renaissance background for the poetic imitation of a redeemed world. The image of an improved natural world can hardly be maintained without some degree of acceptance of the demands of sensuality. This attitude is presented vividly in the influential 12th century allegory of Alain de Lille, *The Complaint of Nature*, in which the drives of life are praised and encouraged by the personified Natura, but said to be perverted by man. Natura visits man from "the inner palace of the impassable heavens", in the figure of a heavenly virgin. She has created man

---

[20] *Divine Weeks,* p. 23.
[21] Sir John Davies, "Of Human Knowledge", *Nosce Teipsum,* in *Works* ed. A. B. Grosart (Edinburgh, 1878), Vol. I, p. 54.
[22] *Ovid's Metamorphosis,* p. 195.
[23] *Poems,* ed. Phyllis Brooks Bartlett (New York, 1941), p. 41.

by bringing "the fluctuating material of the body out from the impure essence of primordial matter into true being". Alain, as the representative of mankind, is ignorant of her mission. Natura replies:

Can it be that thou dost not know that the transgression of the earthly sphere, that the disorder in the ordering of the world, that the carelessness of government, that the unjustness of law, have forced me to descend from the innermost sanctuaries of heavenly mystery to the common brothels of earth? [24]

She describes the completeness of the law of nature, according to which all things "are bound in willing subjection to the inviolability of my commands". Only man "rejects the music of my harp, and raves under the lyre of frenzied Orpheus". This failure to obey the law of nature, Natura observes, is due to the conflict of reason and lustful sensuality in man:

And just as the army of the planets opposes with contrary motion the fixed rolling of the firmament, so in man is found a continual hostility between lust and reason. For the activity of reason, taking its rise from a celestial source, passes through the low levels or earth, and, watchful of heavenly things, turns again to heaven. The activities of lust, on the other hand, wandering waywardly and contrary to the firmament of reason, turn and slip down into the decline of things of earth. Now the latter, lust, leads the human mind into the ruin of vices, so that it perishes; the former, reason, bids it, as it rises, to ascend to the serenity of virtue. The one dishonors man, and changes him to a beast; the other mightily transfigures him into a god.[25]

Natura does not, however, neglect the demands represented by Venus, Hymen, and their son Cupid. But her attitude toward them is one of mixed feelings: "I do not deny the essential nature of love's honorableness if it is checked by the bridle of moderation, if it is restrained by the reins of sobriety, if it does not transgress the determined boundaries of the dual activity, or its heat boil to too great a degree." At first Venus labored energetically in the service of Natura and her law, maintaining the

---

[24] *Complaint, ed. cit.,* pp. 5, 24, 34. The descent of the Attendant Spirit in *Comus* is markedly similar to the descent in this last passage.
[25] *Ibid.,* pp. 35, 36, 26.

fertility of the world. But soon she came more to enjoy being "pampered in unfruitful love than to be exercised in fruitful labors, though she had been trusted ... with the busy work of a festal activity". Venus, a victim of the passions, "began as a concubine, defiling the chastity of her marriage bed". Together with her consort, Antigamus, the enemy of marriage, she produces the illegitimate offspring Mirth, who is contrasted with Cupid, the lawful son of Venus and Hymen. A "solemn marriage" accounts for the birth of Cupid; a "low and notorious concubinage" for Mirth.[26] Alain attempts to combine in his Natura the demands of the world of spirit, available to man through the rational apprehension of the law of nature, and the demands of sexual love, the regulation of which is delegated to Venus, Hymen, and Cupid. This chaste regulation, ironically, has been perverted by Venus herself, leading Natura to condemn mankind for his submission to the power of lust and his rejection of the natural law.

This balance between the demands of sensuality and the law of nature implied by *The Complaint of Nature* reveals, according to E. R. Curtius, Alain's attempt to move away from the paganism of such a work as Bernard Silvestris' *De universitate mundi* in the direction of orthodox Christian doctrine, although a degree of the "optimistic naturalism" of Bernard is still evident. The function of Alain's Natura, Curtius observes, "must be understood as an attempt to find a place in the divine order for the forces and drives of life".[27] The same effort is considerably more pronounced in the 16th century; what Alain calls the "determined boundaries of the dual activity" of sense and reason becomes the objective for the poetic imitation of a perfected natural world in much of the literature of this period. Alain's personification of nature, through which is expressed the interaction of the natural and divine orders, is paralleled in the 16th century by Spenser's double image of nature in the *Mutabilitie Cantos*: "Then forth issewed (great goddesse) great dame nature" with a veil

> That, some do say, was so by skill devized,
> To hide the terror of her uncouth hew

[26] *Ibid.*, pp. 49, 55.
[27] *European Literature*, p. 121.

> From mortall eyes that should be sore agrized;
> For that her face did like a Lion shew,
> That eye of wight could not indure to view:
> But others tell that it so beautious was,
> And round about such beames of splendor threw,
> That it the Sunne a thousand times did pass,
> Ne could be seene but like an image in a glass.[28]

The beauty and ugliness of this figure provides an image of nature which is, on one hand, a function of the divine world, and on the other, a condition of destructive sensuality. This two-faced nature of Spenser's reflects his equivocation concerning the problem of "finding a place in the divine order for the forces and drives of life". It is an equivocation, however, calculated to express poetically a particular relationship between the values of both worlds; a relationship which forms a balance between what reason permits and what nature demands. That imagined natural world which this balance characterizes is a redeemed nature, purified of the corruptions of sensuality but not of sensuality itself.

That realignment of the natural and the spiritual, that perfection of nature in the direction of the divine world which identifies the scheme of the redemption of nature, may be imitated in Renaissance poetry through the conflict and reconciliation of sense and reason, for in these two capacities the values of both worlds are expressed. The tension in nature between the corrupting and the redeeming centers in bi-form man, who is part brute and part god. It is his responsibility to establish a condition in which the lowest and highest levels of nature may exist in harmony. Nature, then, is potentially redeemable, and man has the capacity for acting as the agent of redemption. Such a conception of the destiny of man indicates not only a shift in the scene of salvation from heaven to earth, but a shift in the agent from Christ to man. In the poetic imitation of a redeemed world the acts of restoration are not, however, accomplished without the aid of forces from the upper world.

---

[28] *The Faerie Queene*, 7.6.5-6.

C. VENUS AND DIANA

It has been suggested that a particular conflict between the natural and the spiritual worlds provides the necessary foundation for the poetic expression of the reconciliation of those two worlds in terms of a perfected rather than a transcended nature. The conflict is between the eternal world of divine order and purity, and the mutable world which in its lowest state is seen to be disordered and corrupting. The influence of the divine upon the natural, the eternal upon the mutable, raises the condition of nature into an alignment with the world of spirit, but does not negate its mutability or renounce its values. The achievement of this balance and the conflict which leads to it, as imitated in Renaissance poetry, provides the content of the poetic theme of the redemption of nature. In addition, it has been asserted that the polarity of sense and reason is a representation, in a more limited way, of the polarity of nature and spirit. The sensual, in the tradition of thought involved here, is associated with that disordered and corrupt dimension of nature. The reason, on the other hand, is a human capacity which is associated with and reveals the impress of the world of spirit. The control of the sensual by the rational raises the level of nature in the direction of the divine. The new condition of nature is the result of an attempt to account for rather than reject the forces and drives of life in their relation to the divine order.

The objective in this section is to provide outlines for another polarity which is also a representation, in a more limited way, of the nature-spirit conflict. This other polarity, which further restricts the range of discussion here, is that between Venus and Diana, or between sexual passion and sexual purity. It is a conflict which presents a specific aspect of the larger polarity of sense and reason. From the point of view of the four-fold universe referred to above, the sexual passions are, in the unredeemed world, located in the lowest dimension of nature, and therefore associated with the eternal world of the demonic. The idea of purity reflects the impress of the divine upon the natural world because in poetry it is an image of the total renunciation of nature. A reconciliation of these two contradictory aspects of experience, in which the value of passion is modified by purity and the value of purity by passion, provides an effective dramatic image of the perfection of nature. The reason for this is that the erotic most precisely represents those forces in nature which need to be redeemed, and the virginal most precisely represents those values of the divine world which must be impressed upon nature in order to redeem it. Since the poetry which is concerned with the inclusion of the drives of nature in a larger and more perfect order concentrates upon the natural rather than the spiritual world, a compromise between the erotic and the virginal is required. Such a compromise is, so to speak, an agreeable adjustment of the mutual claims of Venus and Diana. In its most unadorned form it is an argument for erotic love governed by chastity and sanctified by the sacrament of marriage. It is what might be called "chaste desire" – a phrase which defines the reconciliation of contradictory aspects of experience, and of contradictory levels of that figurative four-fold universe. In short, this equilibrium between passion and purity may function in poetry as an elaborate metaphor for a perfected or redeemed nature.

It is not the intention here to treat exhaustively the configurations of this metaphor in Renaissance poetry, but rather to concentrate on single works of Spenser, Shakespeare, and Milton, which are representative of this poetic tradition, in order to demonstrate how the conflict and reconciliation of passion and purity may stand for the process and achievement of a perfected natural world. Before undertaking these analyses, however, it is necessary to provide in more detail the terms of the conflict and the nature of some of the solutions to it.

A common attitude of the age concerning the opposition between the passionate and the pure is exemplified by one of the discussions which occur in Sir John Davies' *Orchestra* (1596). Penelope, the chaste queen of Ulysses, and Antinous, a "fresh and jolly knight", are engaged in a dispute over dancing. Antinous, after praising dance for a number of stanzas, concludes his argument in this manner:

Lo, this is Dancing's true nobility:
Dancing, the child of Music and of Love;
Dancing itself, both love and harmony,
Where all agree and all in order move;
Dancing, the art, that all arts do approve;
   The fair character of the world's consent,
   The heav'n's true figure, and th' earth's ornament.[29]

Penelope, who has been waiting for an opportunity to refute
Antinous, answers that Love, the parent of Dancing, is "Of every
ill the hateful father vile". Love is, for Penelope, "Cunningly
mad, religiously profane, / Wit's monster, reason's canker, sense's
bane" (680 ff.). Love has taught men dancing, and dancing is
an art

   . . . that showeth th' idea of his mind
   With vainness, frenzy, and misorder fraught.

                   (695-6)

Penelope has, in her answer, opposed Antinous' equation of
dance, love, harmony, order, and the image of heaven, with her
own equation linking love and dance with disorder, madness, the
profanation of religion, and the disease of reason. It is a familiar
dialectic between sense and reason, passion and purity, and,
ultimately, between a decayed nature and a nature which reveals
the universal law. For Antinous, love and dance fulfill this *lex
aeterna,* while for Penelope, of course, these activities break the
law. The resolution of the dispute is made rhetorically rather
than dramatically. Antinous accuses Penelope of confusing "Love
the innocent" with "mischievous Lust, which traitorously /
Usurps his name and steals his ornament" (710-11). True love, as opposed to lust,

   Is he that tuned the world's whole harmony,
   And linked all men in sweet society.

                 (713-14)

He concludes by drawing a grand parallel between love and
concord:

   Concord's true picture shineth in this art,
   Where divers men and women ranked be,

[29] Ll. 666-72, in *Poetry of the English Renaissance,* ed. J. W. Hebel
and H. H. Hudson (New York, 1929), p. 350.

And everyone doth dance a several part,
Yet all as one in measure do agree,
Observing perfect uniformity;
    All turn together, all together trace,
    And all together honor and embrace.

If they whom sacred Love hath linked in one
Do as they dance, in all their course of life,
Never shall burning grief nor bitter moan
Nor factious difference nor unkind strife
Arise between the husband and the wife.

                                            (764-75)

The passage becomes rather Platonic after this as Penelope's "ravished mind in heav'nly thoughts did dwell" (853), and Terpsichore is replaced by Urania for inspiration on another level. Although a divine love is eventually the subject here, the contention between Antinous and Penelope does reveal a significant pattern of paralleled oppositions: order-disorder, reason-sense, love-lust, and concord-discord. Larger cosmic polarities have their correspondence in the more immediate conflicts of human life.

Antinous, of course, is not a type of the evil seducer whose argument for love and pleasure is meant to be specious. Penelope, certainly, is suspicious of his motives; but when he formulates the equation between love and the universal order the taint to his position vanishes. The evil seducer is normally involved in a different kind of contention, one in which the unavoidable demands of nature come into conflict with the denials of such demands by a chaste hero or heroine. The arguments of the allegorical figure of Pleasure in Carew's masque, *Coelum Britannicum*, and of Phaedria and Acrasia in *The Faerie Queene*, may serve as examples of this more demonic kind of persuasion to love and pleasure.

Lady Hedone, or Pleasure, in Carew's masque, offers a corruption of the classical Epicurean argument:

Beyond me nothing is; I am the goal,
The journey's end, to which the sweating world
And wearied Nature travels. For this, the best

And wisest sect of all philosophers
Made me the seat of supreme happiness . . .

My necessary offices preserve
Each single man, and propagate the kind.
Then am I universal, as the light,
Or common air we breathe.[30]

At the conclusion of her speech, an antimasque of the five senses
is introduced:

> Come forth, my subtle organs of delight!
> With changing figures please the curious eye,
> And charm the ear with moving harmony.
>
> (805-7)

The counter-argument comes from Mercury, who, in pointing out
the evilness of Lady Hedone, does not wholly condemn the demands of the senses. For him, Pleasure is a "bewitching Syren,
gilded rottenness", who has artfully presented "Th' enamel'd outside and the honied verge of the fair cup, where deadly poison
lurks".

> Grief is the shadow waiting on thy steps,
> Which, as the joys 'gin tow'rds their west decline
> Doth to a giant's spreading form extend
> Thy dwarfish stature. Thou thyself art Pain,
> Greedy, intense desire, and the keen edge
> Of thy fierce appetite oft strangles thee,
> And cuts they slender thread; but still the terror
> And apprehension of thy hasty end
> Mingles with gall thy most refined sweets:
> Yet thy Circean charms transform the world . . .
>
> Can'st thou then dream, those powers that from heaven have
> Banish'd th' effect, will there enthrone the cause?
> To thy voluptuous den, fly, Witch, from hence!
> There dwell, for ever drown'd in brutish sense.
>
> (815-24; 832-35)

Phaedria, in Book II of *The Faerie Queene*, has her domain in
the "wide Inland sea, that hight by name / The Idle lake". She

[30] Ll. 772-76; 790-93, in *Poems*, ed. Rhodes Dunlap (Oxford, 1949),
pp. 173-74.

exercises her seductive powers on Cymochles, charming him
with a "love lay" of idleness:

> The lilly, Lady of the flowring field,
> The flowre-deluce, her lovely Paramoure,
> Bid thee to them thy fruitlesse labors yield,
> And soone leave off this toylsome weary stoure:
> Loe, loe! how brave she decks her bounteous boure,
> With silkin curtens and gold coverletts,
> Therein to shroud her sumptuous Belamoure;
> Yet nether spinnes nor cardes, ne cares nor fretts,
> But to her mother Nature all her care she letts.
>
> Why then doest thou, O man! that of them all
> Art Lord, and eke of nature Soveraine,
> Wilfully make thyselfe a wretched thrall,
> And waste thy joyous howres in needlesse paine,
> Seeking for daunger and adventures vaine?
> What bootes it all to have, and nothing use?
> Who shall him rew that swimming in the maine
> Will die for thrist, and water doth refuse?
> Refuse such fruitlesse toile, and present pleasures chuse.[31]

Another love lay, sung in the Bowre of Blisse, conveys the attitude of Acrasia, a doctrine similar to Phaedria's in its persuasion
to make use of what nature provides man:

> Ah, see, whoso fayre thing doest faine to see,
> In springing flowre the image of the day.
> Ah! see the Virgin Rose, how sweetly shee
> Doth first peepe forth with bashfull modestee,
> That fairer seemes the lesse ye see her may.
> Lo! see soone after how more bold and free
> Her bared bosome she doth broad display;
> Lo! see soone after how she fades and falls away.
>
> So passeth, in the passing of a day,
> Of mortall life the leafe, the bud, the flowre;
> Ne more doth florish after first decay,
> That earst was sought to deck both bed and bowre
> Of many a lady', and many a Paramowre.
> Gather therefore the Rose whilest yet is time,
> Whilest loving thou mayest loved be with equall crime.
>
> (2.12.74-5)

---

[31] *The Faerie Queene*, 2.6.16-17.

More elaborate expressions of this argument for love and the opposition which rises against it can be found in Marlowe's *Hero and Leander*, and Sidney's *Arcadia*. A greater sense of immediacy is generated in the relevant portions of these works because of a comparatively effective dramatic conflict rather than a simple rhetorical presentation of a debate. The contention in both cases involves a chaste figure in opposition to a representative of the naturalistic doctrine of love. In Marlowe, the persuasions of Leander are eventually successful with Hero; while in Sidney, the argument of Cecropia obviously is included in order that it may be refuted. For this reason there is in Sidney more rhetoric than drama, although, as Harry Levin comments, Leander too seems "better versed in dialectic than blandishment".[32]

Leander's blandishments are directed toward Hero, described as "Venus' nun" – an epithet which reflects her role in the poem as an embodiment of the conflict between experience and innocence, or passion and purity.[33] She is caught between the two worlds of nature and spirit. Her purity links her to the virtuous order of the upper world, and her beauty and desire for Leander link her to that level of nature which may corrupt and imbrute. Leander, in beginning his persuasions to love, insists that his words "shall be as spotless as my youth, / Full of simplicity and naked truth".[34] He appeals to Hero as a "heavenly nymph, beloved of human swains" who being loved "receives no blemish, but ofttimes more grace" (1st sest., 217-18). The conjunction which Leander makes between love and grace, the two prime characteristics of the world of nature and the world of spirit respectively, appears to be a rhetorical trick on his part to convince Hero that a sexual alliance with him will not violate her virtuous alliance with the divine. The core of his argument is the familiar naturalistic doctrine of waste:

> Like untuned golden strings all women are,
> Which long time lie untouched, will harshly jar.
> Vessels of brass, oft handled, brightly shine;

---

[32] *The Overreacher* (Cambridge, Mass., 1952), p. 19.
[33] See *The Overreacher*, p. 19.
[34] First sestiad, ll. 207-8, in *Poetry of the English Renaissance*, pp. 173-4.

> What difference betwixt the richest mine
> And basest mold, but use? for both, not used,
> Are of like worth. Then treasure is abused,
> When misers keep it; being put to loan,
> In time it will return us two for one.
> Rich robes themselves and others do adorn;
> Neither themselves nor others, if not worn.
>
> (1st sest., 229-38)

Once he establishes that maidens have no value "without the sweet society of men", Leander begins his attack upon virginity. First of all, it is only an appearance:

> This idol which you term virginity
> Is neither essence subject to the eye,
> No, nor to any one exterior sense,
> Nor hath it any place of residence,
> Nor is't of earth or mould celestial,
> Or capable of any form at all.
>
> (1st sest., 269-74)

It is foolish to boast of something "which hath no being"; and how can one lose something that does not exist? Furthermore, Leander argues, it is not logical to call virginity a virtue because we are born in that condition; virtue and honor are "purchased by the deeds we do". Hero, as a nun of Venus, is betraying that goddess with her cold attitude:

>   ... The rites
> In which love's beauteous empress most delights
> Are banquets, Doric music, midnight revel,
> Plays, masks, and all that stern age counteth evil.
> Thee as a holy idiot doth she scorn,
> For thou, in vowing chastity, hast sworn
> To rob her name and honor, and thereby
> Commit'st a sin far worse than perjury,
> Even sacrilege against her deity,
> Through regular and formal purity.
>
> (1st sest., 299-308)

Only when her "sweet rites are performed and done" will Hero fulfill her role as a nun of Venus.

Hero, according to Marlowe, had long since "swallowed Cupid's golden hook"; and thus while answering Leander with angry words, her "looks yielded". She

> Strove to resist the motions of her heart;
> And hands so pure, so innnocent, nay such
> As might have made stoop to have a touch,
> Did she uphold to Venus, and again
> Vowed spotless chastity, but all in vain.
>
> (1st sest., 364-68)

A more athletic contention now follows in which Hero, "seeming lavish, saved her maidenhead". The lovers part, each with tokens: Hero with a purple ribbon, and Leander with a sacred ring of Hero's "wherewith she was endowed, / When first religious chastity she vowed". Marlowe's poem ends with the submission, finally, of Hero to Leander when the lovers are reunited after Leander's swim across the Hellespont.

In spite of the rhetorical nature of Leander's argument in the poem, which gives the impression that a specious link is made between the demands of love and the demands of grace in order that Hero may be persuaded to love, there is a rather vivid presentation of a real issue confronting the heroine. Although the issue is expressed in a somewhat gaudy manner, it is clear that some kind of alliance between the two extreme demands is necessary for her to solve the conflict between, on one hand, her beauty and passion, and, on the other, her vow of a "regular and formal purity". That the alliance ultimately seems to be unholy does not invalidate the substance of the conflict or the importance of such a solution. The chaste heroine with a problem of this kind supplies one of the most significant patterns of action for the theme of the redemption of nature. The conflicting demands of the worlds of nature and spirit exist in tension around and within such a heroine. If a resolution of this tension is to be made within rather than beyond nature, it is necessary that the values of beauty and desire be accounted for as well as the value of purity. Such a compromise purifies passion of its demonic aspects and binds it to the purity of the chaste heroine. This action, which perfects the natural world, accounts in part for the theme of the redemption of nature. The chaste heroine can be

seen as a type of bi-form man, a figure who may submit wantonly
to her passions, or retain her "regular and formal purity". In the
kind of reconciliation between the natural and the spiritual with
which I am here concerned, the chaste heroine characteristically
does neither; her objective, like nature's itself, is to "find a place
in the divine order for the forces and drives of life".

Although it is the Pamela-Cecropia episode which presents the
conflict between these two attitudes toward love most fully in the
Arcadia, there are other portions of that work in which aspects
of the issue are involved.[35] First of all, the praise of feminine
beauty in a song by Pyrocles, which is meant as a celebration of
the beauty of Philoclea, the object of his love, can be contrasted
with old Miso's lecture against Cupid. Pyrocles reveals himself
as a servant of Cupid by his delight in the flesh:

> So good assay invites the eye,
> A little downward to espy,
> The lively clusters of her breasts,
> Of Venus babe the wanton nests:
> Like pomels round of marble clear;
> Where azur'd veins well mix'd appear,
> With dearest tops of porphyrie.
>   Betwixt these two a way doth lie,
> A way more worthy of beauty's fame,
> Than that which bears the Milky name.
> This leads into the joyous field,
> Which only still doth lillies yield:
> But lillies such whose native smell,
> The Indian odors doth excel.
> Waist it is called, for it doth waste
> Men's lives, until it be embrac'd.[36]

---

[35] The entire *Arcadia* has been interpreted as an expression in a variety
of dramatic incidents of the general pattern of "private Passion causing
public chaos, often involving the misuse of love". See Walter R. Davis,
"Thematic Unity in the new *Arcadia*", *Studies in Philology*, LVII (1960),
123-43.
[36] Book II, *The Countess of Pembroke's Arcadia*, ed. Ernest A. Baker
(London, 1907), p. 181. Pyrocles' song may be read as an expression of
the sin of *curiositas* (lust of the eyes) which is condemned in the Christian
ascetic tradition as one aspect of the libidinous triplex of *libido sentiendi,
libido sciendi,* and *libido dominandi.* See appendix D, "Libido", in Levin,
The Overreacher, pp. 176-8.

The old woman, Miso, on the other hand, scolds her audience
of Pamela, Philoclea, and Pyrocles (disguised as the Amazon
Zelmene) for their "tittle-tattlings of Cupid", and proceeds to
relate a story of her youth in which she tells of an old woman
who once showed her a picture of Cupid as a foul and ugly
monster. "Could such a thing come from the belly of fair Venus?"
the younger Miso asked, whereupon the old woman presented
her with some verses on Cupid, which Miso now passes on to
the young ladies. In these verses Cupid is depicted as a figure
with

> A horned head, cloven feet, and thousand eyes,
>   Some gazing still, some winking wily shifts,
> Whose long large ears, where never rumour dies.
>   His horned head doth seem the heaven to spite,
>   His cloven foot doth never tread aright.
> Thus half a man, with man he daily haunts,
>   Cloth'd in the shape which soonest may deceive:
> Thus half a beast, each beastly vice he plants,
>   In those weak hearts that his advice receive.[37]

The enthusiastic sensuality of Pyrocles may be contrasted with
the anti-love doctrine of Miso. The two passages function in the
Arcadia as a simple opposition between a concept of sexual
pleasure which is demanded by nature, and a concept of sexual
pleasure which is said to corrupt and imbrute mankind.

This simple opposition is complicated in Amphailus' dream in
Book III of the *Arcadia*, for in this episode an attempt is made
at a reconcilement between innocence and experience, or Diana
and Venus. The conception of love as brutish and evil, which
would be most suitable to the condition of innocence, and the
conception of love as the ultimate in sensual pleasure, which
would be most suitable to the condition of experience, need to
be gently yoked together to produce a new whole. This objective

[37] Miso of course is describing Pan; but it seems to be in the interests
of her anti-love doctrine that the gods of nature and love be equated. She
exploits the bestial elements in her allegory of this aspect of human experience. Compare Miso's interpretation of Pan's horns with that of
Sandys and Bacon. The Miso lecture can be found in *Arcadia, ed. cit.*,
pp. 196-8.

is the aim of Amphialus' dream. He falls asleep in a state of mind pure and free of "base desire". He is transported in his dream to an ideal landscape; in this condition he grows introspective:

> ... there I was, and there my calmy thoughts I fed
> On nature's sweet repast, as healthful senses led.
> Her gifts my study was, her beauty were my sport,
> My work her works to know, her dwelling my resort.
> Those lamps of heav'nly fire to fixed motion bound,
> The ever turning spheres, the never moving ground;
> What essence destiny hath, if fortune be or no;
> Whence our immortal souls to mortal earth do flow:
> What life it is, and how that all these lives do gather,
> With outward maker's force, or like an inward father.
> Such thoughts, methought, I thought, and strain'd my single mind.

These questions concerning whether man's life is immortal or mortal, whether man is subject to his own will or God's, prepare Amphialus' mind for the vision of the goddesses Venus and Diana and the virgin Mira which follows. Diana speaks first to Venus:

> I know full well you know, what discord long hath reign'd
> Betwixt us two; how much that discord foul hath stain'd
> Both our estates, while each the other did deprave ...
> Our names are quite forgot, our temples are defac'd;
> Our offerings spoil'd, our priests from priesthood are displac'd.
> But let us wiser be; and what foul discord brake,
> So much more strong again let fastest concord make ...
> Let one the princess be, to her the other yield:
> For vain equality is but contention's field.
> And let her have the gifts that should in both remain;
> In her let beauty both, and chasteness fully reign.

Diana then proposes that Amphialus choose "which of us two is she, / To whom precedence shall of both accorded be". The proposition pleases Venus, for she feels that her beauty will lead Amphialus to choose her. They both speak at once, attempting to persuade Amphialus in his decision. Their boldness and pride anger him and he awards the double crown to the virgin Mira. The goddesses accuse Amphialus of betrayal. Venus vows to make him burn with desire for Mira, and Diana promises "the chasteness I will give, / In ashes of despair, though burnt, shall make thee live". The attempted reconcilement of desire and

purity in Mira appears to be a failure, for the angered goddesses
have made sure that their opposite demands shall remain in
conflict. The nature of the resolution, however, is clear. Mira is
a projection of Amphialus' imagination who combines in an ideal
mixture the purity of innocence and the sensuality of experience.
By means of the three female figures in this dream, then, is
presented a relatively complex image of the dramatic tension between passion and purity, and its possible resolution.[38]

Philocles and Pamela, the two young ladies who are destined
to be matched with Pyrocles and Musidorus, are, in the course
of the action of the *Arcadia*, captured by the witch-like Cecropia
and imprisoned in her castle. It is Cecropia's fervent wish that
one of these sisters should marry her son. She exercises her
persuasions first on Philoclea, who has vowed eternal chastity.
"The heavens prevent such a mischief", Cecropia claims. "A vow
quoth you? No, no, my dear niece, nature, when you were first
born, vowed you a woman, and as she made you a child of a
mother, so to do your best to be mother of a child: She gave you
beauty to move love; she gave you wit to know love; she gave
you an excellent body to reward love; which kind of liberal re-
warding is crowned with unspeakable felicity." These persuasions
fall upon deaf ears, and Cecropia finds it necessary to seek out
Pamela. In beginning her campaign with Pamela, Cecropia develops her ideas about beauty:

Beauty, beauty, dear niece, is the crown of the feminine greatness;
which gift on whomsoever the heavens ... do bestow, without question, she is bound to use it to the noble purpose for which it is
created.

Pamela replies:

I fear you will make me not only think myself fairer than ever I did,
but think my fairness a matter of greater value than heretofore I could
imagine it. For I ever, till now, conceived those conquests you speak
of rather to proceed from the weakness of the conquered than from
the strength of the conquering power; as they say, the Cranes over-
throw whole battles of Pigmies, not so much of their cranish courage,
as because the other are Pigmies. ... But since your older years, and

[38] Amphialus' dream may be found in *Arcadia, ed. cit.,* pp. 331-35.

abler judgment find beauty to be worthy of so incomparable esti-
mation, certainly, methinks, it ought to be held in dearness, according
to the excellency, and no more than we would do of things which
we account precious, never to suffer it to be defiled.

Cecropia immediately objects to the word defile, arguing that
beauty is to be joined to love and in that way it is honored not
defiled. She attempts to persuade Pamela with a *carpe diem*
argument:

Do you see how the spring-time is full of flowers, decking itself with
them, and not aspiring to the fruits of autumn? what lesson is that
unto you, but that in the April of your age, you should be like April?
let not some of them for whom already the grave gapeth, and perhaps
envy the felicity in you, which themselves cannot enjoy, persuade you
to loose the hold of occasion, while it may not only be taken, but
offers, nay sues to be taken, which if it be not now taken, will never
hereafter be overtaken.

Sidney remarks that it is Cecropia's purpose to make Pamela
"less feeling of those heavenly conceits, that then she might easily
wind her to her crooked bias". Thus, Cecropia levels a direct and
forceful attack on those divine sanctions with which Pamela associates herself: "Fear, and indeed foolish fear, and fearful ignorance, was the first inventor of those conceits; for when they
heard it thunder, not knowing the natural cause, they thought
there was some angry body above that spake so loud."

. . . so as it is manifest enough that all things follow but the course of
their own nature, saving only man, who while by the pregnancy of
his imagination he strives to things supernatural, meanwhile he loseth
his own natural felicity. Be wise, and that wisdom shall be a God unto
thee; be contented, and that is thy heaven.

Pamela, "whoose cheeks were dyed in the beautifullest grain of
virtuous anger", replies to this argument with a lengthy and
learned demonstration of the existence of a divine order throughout the entire cosmos, and therefore of the existence of God.
"Perfect order, perfect beauty, perfect constancy" cannot be the
work of chance. Anticipating a counter-argument from Cecropia
to the effect that this order "is so by nature", Pamela affirms the
necessity of a supreme wisdom which makes all things concur:

This world therefore cannot otherwise consist but by a mind of wisdom, which governs it; which whether you will allow to be the creator thereof, as undoubtedly he is, or the soul and governor thereof, most certain it is, that whether he govern all, or make all, his power is above either his creatures, or his government.

Although Pamela's discourse does not directly counter Cecropia's naturalistic arguments for the fulfillment of "natural felicity", her doctrine does, in effect, align her with that dimension of nature which reveals the impress of the divine law, and therefore distinguishes her from the corrupting claims of nature expressed by Cecropia. Pamela, however chaste, is still a love heroine, and does not avoid desire. Like Amphialus she requires a reconcilement of the claims of Venus and Diana. She carves this couplet upon a tree:

> Sweet root say thou, the root of my desire
> Was virtue clad in constant love's attire.

In Sidney's own term, a "virtuous wantonness" characterizes this heroine; and in a variety of passages in the *Arcadia* the conflict between Venus and Diana, reason and sense, innocence and experience, purity and passion, the "naturalistic" and the law of nature, is meant to be resolved in an equilibrium of the contradictory demands. The figure of Mira provides a simple and clear image of this balance. She is an idealized mortal, not a goddess; but Amphialus wants to combine in her the qualities of both Venus and Diana. In Mira "let beauty both, and chasteness fully reign." Such an image of the union of the highest and lowest reaches of nature may stand as a metaphor for a nature perfected by the harmony between the elements of the upper and lower worlds.[39]

---

[39] The Pamela-Cecropia episode may be found in *Arcadia, ed. cit.*, pp. 319-23, 337-45. See also the epithalamium, pp. 505-7, for Sidney's concept of the resolution of the conflict discussed in these paragraphs. For information on the sources and interpretation of this episode, see: Edwin Greenlaw, "The Captivity Episode in Sidney's Arcadia", *Manly Anniversary Papers* (Chicago, 1923), pp. 54-63; Lois Whitney, "Concerning Nature in *The Countesse of Pembroke's Arcadia*", *Studies in Philology*, XXIV (1927), 207-22; Constance M. Syford, "The Direct Source of the Pamela-Cecropia Episode in the *Arcadia*", *PMLA*, XLIX (1934), 472-89.

The naturalistic arguments in the works briefly examined above are placed in rhetorical or dramatic tension with the arguments for purity and true love. The characters from the lower level of nature emphasize the "naturalness" of desire, that the commodity of beauty must be used in order to be fulfilled, that time destroys beauty so that it may never be fulfilled, and that "natural felicity" should not be renounced in favor of some superstitious fear of the supernatural. By placing these rebellious arguments in a position in which they are obviously meant to be proven false and evil, the "purity", so to speak, of the naturalist's position is considerably weakened. Even in *Hero and Leander*, the most militant expression of the rightness of naturalistic doctrine, the portrayal of Hero as a nun of Venus and her chaste misgivings about the persuasions of Leander tend to qualify the positive force of the total "emancipation of the flesh" for which the poem appears to argue. In the Renaissance *carpe diem* lyric tradition, however, the naturalistic persuasions to love and the seizure of beauty are presented with virtually no opposition, only the off-stage protestations of the coy maiden. There is, then, in these lyrics, an excellent opportunity for the argument of love to be expressed without contradiction. There is no conflict within the structure of these poems between the claims of two worlds; the *carpe diem* world is devoted wholly to nature.

A brief examination of such unhindered statements of the position of naturalism is relevant to the discussion here, for that realignment of the natural with the spiritual which constitutes the redemption of nature includes the satisfaction of sexual desire and the fulfillment of beauty. The poetic aim of this kind of lyric is to isolate a perfect moment of beauty and pleasure, and to argue that this moment must be seized or fulfilled before it passes, for it will never come again. This is an attempt to establish an "eternal present" in which nature is in her prime, and therefore ripe for complete fulfillment. The need to create a condition of absolute perfection within the natural world is a naturalistic and secular counterpart of the need in the orthodox Christian tradition to transcend the world of nature in order that a condition of absolute perfection may be reached in the world of spirit. The ironic relationship between these two states of perfection or "salvation" is significant to the discussion of the theme of order here because the *carpe diem* perfection or "redemption" of nature is accomplished without any alignment between the natural and the spiritual; the two worlds are related only in the most ironic way.

First of all, the *carpe diem* lyric reveals a high degree of sensitivity to the mutations of the natural world. This is a concern of the age which obviously need not be the special possession of those who devalue the natural world and advocate a heavenly goal for man. It may also be the concern of those who are sensitive to the instability of human life and its aims, and advocate some positive human action in order to "devour time" before the possibilities of life are themselves devoured. Love of the world as well as *contemptu mundi* may abhor mutability. The defeat of this mutability may be the aim of those who exalt as well as those who vilify nature. The fixity and purity of the heavenly goal has its naturalistic parallel in the moment to be seized in *carpe diem* poetry. In both instances mutability is overcome (from the point of view of poetic intention); in the first because of submission to a perfection of earthly pleasure, and in the second because of a rejection and transcendence of that pleasure. Both answers to the decay of nature are poetic affirmations which provide extremes to the theme of the redemption of nature I am exploring here. In the first case a perfected natural world is figuratively expressed in the moment of beauty and pleasure to be seized; in the second a perfected condition is figuratively expressed by the transcendence of the natural in favor of the heavenly.

The most evident intention of the *carpe diem* lyric is to persuade a maid to seize, together with the poet, this moment of pleasure in a world of passing beauty. In Herrick's "To the Virgins, To Make Much of Time", the persuasion develops from a series of strongly opposed conditions: blooming flower-dying flower, rising sun-setting sun, youth-age, and prime beauty-decayed beauty.

> Gather ye rose buds while ye may,
>   Old time is still a-flying,

And this same flower that smiles to-day,
  To-morrow will be dying.

The glorious lamp of heaven, the sun,
  The higher he's a-getting,
The sooner will his race be run,
  And nearer he's to setting.

That age is best which is the first,
  When youth and blood are warmer;
But being spent, the worse, and worst
  Times still succeed the former.

Then be not coy, but use your time,
  And while ye may, go marry;
For having lost but once your prime,
  Ye may forever tarry.

These opposed conditions, however, are not strict polarities, for
the flower is not yet dead, the sun is not yet set, age and death
have not yet succeeded youth, and the maiden need not allow
her beauty to decay. Rather than a sharp break between each
alternative in these paralleled conditions, an incipient perfection
is suggested. This poise between unrealized growth and final
decay serves to isolate the very moment to be seized. It is not,
however, a temporal moment. It is that impossible time when
the life of the flower or the maid has reached fruition and not
yet begun to decay. The moment has "a quality of suspension . . .
defining an eternal prolongation of the state just prior to fulfillment".[40] The nature of the moment is made even clearer in Daniel's Sonnet XXXI to Delia:

Look, Delia how we 'steem the half-blown rose,
The image of thy blush and summer's honor,
Whilst in her tender green she doth inclose
That pure sweet beauty time bestows upon her.
No sooner spreads her glory in the air
But straight her full-blown pride is in declining.[41]

[40] Kenneth Burke, "Symbolic Action in a Poem by Keats", *Essays in
Modern Literary Criticism,* ed. Ray B. West, Jr. (New York, 1952), p. 399.
[41] *The Golden Hind,* eds. Roy Lamson and Hallett Smith (New York,
1942), p. 208.

Of primary interest in these lines is the balance that Daniel suggests between the half-blown and the full-blown rose. Within the half-blown rose's greenness resides a "pure sweet beauty", but when the rose becomes full-blown it begins to decline. This incipient purity, which suggests a kind of Christian-Platonic perfection, tends to bring the naturalism of *carpe diem* attitudes into an ironic alignment with the attitudes of the orthodox tradition. The difference, of course, is that two very different roads lead to these ironically similar "ideal" conditions. In *carpe diem* poetry it is temporal experience or sensual "knowledge" which enables one to grasp this moment of absolute perfection. In the religious tradition the union of man with the perfection of the divine is achieved spiritually, by transcending the temporal and sensual. In *carpe diem* poetry the recommended seizure of the moment is a representation of the desire to act in a manner which will fix a point in the mutable world by experiencing the full potential of life. The fixity is, paradoxically, a "temporary stasis", for the sexual satisfaction, or even the beauty of the maid and the rose, is of necessity a passing experience, and therefore unlike the changeless state that is meant to be conveyed by a representation of a spiritual union. The eternal present, then, is an imaginative concept employed in *carpe diem* poetry in order to provide for the defeat of a decaying nature by isolating a moment of temporal existence in its perfection and advocating its seizure and thus fulfillment.

The value of the present moment is looked at from a different perspective by those who emphasize a supernatural salvation for man, yet Jeremy Taylor in *Holy Living and Dying* (1650-51) describes the present in much the same way as the *carpe diem* poet:

... we must, with all arts of the spirit, seize upon the present, because it passes from us while we speak, and because in it all our certainty does consist. We must take our waters as out of a torrent and sudden shower, which will quickly cease dropping from above, and quickly cease running in our channels here below: this instant will never return again, and yet, it may be, this instant will declare or secure the fortune of a whole eternity. ... For he that by a present and constant holiness secures the present, and makes it useful to his noblest purposes, he turns his condition into his best advantages, by making his unavoidable fate become his necessary religion. . . . Since we stay not here, being people of but a day's abode . . . we must look somewhere else for an abiding city, a place in another country to fix our house in, whose walls and foundation is God, where we must find rest, or else be restless forever.[42]

There is a certain amount of ambiguity to this moment as Taylor describes it, but it is clear enough that it is to be used as a kind of viaticum for the fixity and rest man is to find in God. It is also clear that Taylor ultimately rejects the immediate importance of the present moment in favor of its eternal reward. However, he is interested in securing "a whole eternity" in a way strikingly similar to that of *carpe diem* poetry. The concern with mutability and the somewhat desperate seizure of the present are evident in both cases. The crucial difference is that, for Taylor, the fulfillment of man occurs after and beyond the use of the present, while in *carpe diem* poetry the fulfillment of man (and nature) is fixed in the present moment itself. In the first instance, eternity in God is a consequence of a virtuous seizure of the present; in the second, the characteristics of eternity reside within the very moment to be seized. Boethius has given us a classic definition of eternity: ". . . that which grasps and possesses wholly and simultaneously the fulness of unending life, which lacks naught of the future, and has lost naught of the fleeting past . . ."[43] This description appied to heaven may also be applied to that moment in the *carpe diem* lyric in which all the forms of nature have reached their perfection – neither half-blown nor decaying.

Given the assumption that nature is wasted if its beauty is not used (enjoyed), the *carpe diem* lyric expresses the fulfillment of nature in the implied seizure of a temporal moment of perfect beauty. In addition, this fulfillment of nature is an ironic counterpart to the fulfillment of man beyond nature in the City of God. It is, however, a vision of a perfected nature which does not include any vestige of the impress of the divine world; which,

---

[42] (London, 1850), pp. 310-11. See Fredelle Bruser, "*Comus* and the Rose Song", *Studies in Philology*, XLIV (1947), 625-44.
[43] *The Consolation of Philosophy* (New York, The Modern Library, 1943), p. 116.

therefore, distinguishes it from that vision of the order of nature relevant to this study. In spite of this distinction, the naturalism of the *carpe diem* lyric, which has as its foundation the belief that the enjoyment of beauty is the aim of life and that sexual love accomplishes this aim, provides an important dimension to that metaphor of the order of nature which consists of the alignment of the natural and the spiritual. Although the claims of Diana do not function in the *carpe diem* lyric, the claims of Venus govern much of its attitude. These claims eventually must be included in the vision of the redeemed natural world under consideration.

The particularization in this chapter from nature and spirit, to sense and reason, and finally to Venus and Diana, is meant to focus the entire set of ideas on the contention between passion and purity. They are two qualities which in their conflict reveal the interaction of the worlds of nature and spirit, and which in their reconciliation reveal the harmonious alignment of those two worlds. The Renaissance double view of nature, in which the natural world is seen to be linked to the hellish at one end and to the heavenly at the other, affords the possibility, in poetry, of imitating a nature in which the two dimensions become one. In the same way, the conception of man as *compositum mixtum*, able to descend to the brute or rise to the angel, affords the possibilty of expressing the fulfillment of man's rightful potential. The aim of man and nature, in this poetic theme, is not the heavenly city, but the establishment of a world of nature which retains its values of "natural felicity", yet is purified of the corrupting influences of sensuality by the forces of the divine world working within the natural.

II. THE IMITATION OF NATURE

A. FIGURALISM AND SECULARISM

The Renaissance intellectual effort to coordinate those two ranges of experience which are identified in the worlds of nature and spirit is manifest in the symbolic world of its poetry. That fourfold conception of the universe in which the two dimensions of nature reveal the influence of the eternally demonic world below and the eternally divine world above provides a range of poetic images by which a natural world purified of the demonic and aligned with the divine may be imitated. Although in this Renaissance view of reality a commerce between nature and the divine is the objective, the emphasis is placed on the natural rather than the spiritual. It is an attempt to redeem rather than to vilify and transcend nature. The conflict which leads to this perfected natural condition, therefore, concentrates upon the two levels of nature, for within them functions the corruptions of the demonic world and the purities of the heavenly world. The ultimate goal is to redeem the sensuality which characterizes the lower level of nature, and to allow it a place in the upper level, providing a single level of nature which is intimately bound to the divine world but not overcome by it. In this condition there is no longer any opposition between levels of nature; the conception of nature governed by a set of laws which have their origin in the eternal order of the world of spirit is fulfilled. In the poetic representation of this perfected nature and the tension between the two levels of nature which precedes it, the fictional scene is, necessarily, the world of nature; but within this scene the influences of the eternal upper and lower worlds are also represented, attempting to pull man up toward the angels or down toward the brutes. The poetic scene in which this theme of redemption takes form is a natural world in which is manifest the demonic and the divine.

This world view which accepts the potential of man and all nature to become perfected or restored fully within the world of temporal human experience is indicative of the shift in emphasis in the Renaissance away from spirit and toward nature as a sufficient setting for the restoration of the fallen condition of the world, and away from Christ and toward man as a sufficient agent of that restoration. Concerning the changes that took place between the Middle Ages and the Renaissance, Herschel Baker, in *The Wars of Truth,* writes: ". . . Europe had shifted its center of intellectual gravity from God to man, from grace to nature, from theology to philosophy, from supernaturalism to naturalism; consequently a readjustment of the objects and methods of knowledge was made inevitable." [1] It is widely recognized now, of course, that it is for the most part inaccurate to argue a sharp break between the Middle Ages and the Renaissance; in the opposition of the religious and the secular, particularly, it appears to be a distortion to characterize the total world view of the Middle Ages as religious and that of the Renaissance as secular.[2] A transfer of emphasis, however, is commonly recognized; it is not so much a transfer from the thoroughly theological to the thoroughly secular, but rather from the theocentric to the anthropocentric. This is simply another way of stating the central observation of the discussion here of the imitation of a redeemed world: much of the poetry of the 16th and 17th centuries reveals a shift in emphasis from spirit to nature – with the important

---

[1] (Cambridge, Mass., 1952), p. 162.

[2] See, for example, Paul Oskar Kristeller, "Humanism and Scholasticism in the Italian Renaissance", *Studies in Renaissance Thought and Letters* (Rome, 1956), pp. 553-83; Johan Huizinga, *The Waning of the Middle Ages* (London, 1924), and "The Problem of the Renaissance", *Men and Ideas* (New York, Meridian Books, 1959), pp. 243-87; and Wallace K. Ferguson, *The Renaissance in Historical Thought* (Cambridge, Mass., 1948). Baker, too, recognizes this error in historical perspective.

qualification that in poetic imitation the world of spirit is not
totally relinquished, but presented in a mitigated way as working
within the natural world.

This transfer of emphasis, insofar as it involves the relationship between nature and grace, is described by Ernst Cassirer in
terms of a contrast between Augustine and Aquinas:

Within the realm of dogma Thomas Aquinas acknowledged the complete authority of Augustine, and Aquinas' doctrine of predestination
differs in no essential respect from that of Augustine. Yet the general
intellectual atmosphere surrounding this doctrine has undergone a
change. The emphasis in the doctrine of grace has passed from
Augustine's 'gratia praeveniens' to the side of 'gratia cooperans'. The
power of grace is not limited, since it still forms the beginning and
the end of the movement which leads man to God. It introduces this
movement and guides it safely to its goal. But between the beginning
and end there is now a middle ground within which natural powers
are recognized as enjoying rights of their own and a relative independence ... the fall did not extinguish in the human will all power
towards good. If its power is weakened and diminished, the will
retains, nevertheless, a natural inclination towards the true and the
good. It is thus the 'regnum naturae' which points the way to the
'regnum gratiae.' Grace does not nullify nature; rather, it raises
nature to its own level, and finally, even above itself. 'Gratia naturam
non tollit, sed perficit.' [3]

A similar distinction is made by Christopher Dawson, for whom
St. Thomas was the first "to break with the old established tradition of oriental spiritualism and Neoplatonic idealism, and to
bring man back into the order of nature".[4] Although Dawson
insists that Augustine's "Latin sense of social and historical
reality led him to do justice to the social and historical elements
that are implicit in the Christian tradition", he nevertheless recognizes that Augustine was dominated by a "nostalgia for the
infinite" which caused him to "turn away from the world of experience towards the eternal vision of transcendent Beings".[5]
Augustine believed in the "intrusion of another and sacred order

---

[3] *The Platonic Renaissance in England* (Austin, Texas, 1953), p. 90. See
also *The Myth of the State* (New York, Anchor Books, 1955), pp. 131-43.
[4] *Progress and Religion* (London, 1933), p. 173.
[5] *Ibid.,* p. 164.

which condemned the present as incurably corrupt and only redeemed by withdrawing from it".[6] It is clear from this that for
Augustine there was no commerce, in any ultimate way, between
nature and spirit. Aquinas believed that "the earthly state and
the City of God are no longer opposite poles; they are related to
each other and complement each other".[7] It is clear from this
that for St. Thomas there was some kind of commerce or continuity between nature and spirit. However, in spite of the fact
that such a continuity qualified the severity with which Augustine
separated the earthly and the heavenly, and that Thomas gave
greater recognition to the *regnum naturae* than did Augustine,
the common goal of both theologians is not altered – the ultimate
transcendence of the temporal, and the permanence of man's
salvation in the realm of the divine. That is, both Augustine and
Thomas presented theocentric views; and although it can be
claimed that Thomas represents a progression in the Middle Ages
from the view of nature as a *massa perditionis* to one in which
the natural powers enjoy rights of their own, a more complete
emancipation of the forces of nature normally is claimed for the
Renaissance. This theocentric world view conceives of the historical process as a movement along a vertical line toward a
"fixed and permanent supra-terrestrial state in eternity". Opposed
to it is the anthropocentric, which views the historical process as
a movement along a horizontal line toward "a more enlightened
and more comfortable existence in time and space".[8] In both
cases a redemption is involved. In the first instance, man is redeemed through Christ in the realm of grace; in the second,
nature itself is redeemed by a human agent who is aligned but
not identified with the world of grace or spirit.

It is, of course, this latter kind of redemption which is relevant
to the Renaissance poetry with which I am concerned. It is the
restoration of nature by man rather than the restoration of man
beyond nature. The changes which this shift from the spiritual

---

[6] Charles E. Raven, *Natural Religion and Christian Theology* (Cambridge, 1953), p. 51.
[7] Cassirer, *The Myth of the State,* p. 143.
[8] Haydn, *The Counter-Renaissance,* pp. 29-30.

to the natural destiny of man worked upon the literary representation of reality from the Middle Ages to the Renaissance is, in
large part, the subject of Erich Auerbach's *Mimesis*. The gradual
movement from what Auerbach calls a "figural" representation
of reality in the direction of a "secular" representation of reality
corresponds to that shift in historical perspective which first
placed the destiny of man along a vertical line reaching to eternity, and then along a horizontal line leading to the fulfillment
of life within time and space. Figural reality in literature represents a commerce between nature and spirit, but it is a reality in
which the divine ultimately transcends and fulfills the earthly.
Secular reality represents the total sufficiency of the temporal
world for the fulfillment of human life. The Renaissance poetry
which has as its theme what I have defined as the redemption of
nature represents a reality which is no longer figural, but which
is not so thoroughly secular that the impress of the eternal order
is disallowed in the world of nature. A closer examination of
Auerbach's thesis will help to establish more firmly the nature
of that Renaissance poetic world in which supernatural and natural elements combine to express the perfection of the world of
human experience.

The Christian conception of history in which the temporal
event found its fulfillment only beyond history placed certain
requirements of interpretation upon Old Testament scripture in
order to establish a conformity between it and the scripture of
the Christian world view. Auerbach comments on this kind of
interpretation in an earlier essay, "Figura".

Figural interpretation establishes a connection between two events or
persons, the first of which signifies not only itself but also the second,
while the second encompasses or fulfills the first. The two poles of
the figure are separate in time, but both, being real events or figures,
are within time, within the stream of historical life.[9]

Although both events are historically real, the second fulfilling
the first, there is "something provisional and incomplete about

[9] *Scenes from the Drama of European Literature* (New York, Meridian
Books, 1959), p. 53. For the following references to "Figura" see p. 58-60,
72.

them; they point to one another and both point to something in the future, something still to come, which will be the actual, real definitive event". Thus, in the Christian or figural view of reality the actual sensory event loses its immediate significance in time in favor of what it prefigures or promises in the ultimate fulfillment of Christian eschatology. For example, just as Old Testament events prefigure the incarnation, the incarnation itself prefigures or promises "the end of time and the true kingdom of God". In this Christian view, all of history "with all its concrete force, remains forever a figure, cloaked and needful of interpretation". History itself is composed of a series of figural events all leading vertically to ultimate fulfillment in the kingdom of God; no single temporal event contains a sufficiency of value or meaning by itself. Although this attitude toward history subordinates the earthly event and makes it "a part of a wholly divine reality that will be enacted in the future", Auerbach concludes that a figural event is at the same time concrete, tentative, and eternal. It is concrete because it is accepted as historically real; it is tentative because all history is tentative in the sense that it constantly promises ultimate fulfillment; and it is eternal because the eternal reality of the completion of all history in God is prefigured in it. These observations of Auerbach's on a view of reality which accepts an experience of the natural world as empirically actual yet tentatively pointing toward completion beyond nature indicates that within figuralism itself there is a subtle provision for the eventual ascendancy of the natural experience to a position of greater self-sufficiency for the fulfillment of man's destiny.

To this vertical progression of history which has a supernatural fulfillment Auerbach opposes the "modern view of historical development", according to which each natural event has its place in "an unbroken horizontal process", and every occurrence is causally related. Although the final meaning of the causal relationship may be incomplete, each temporal action and agent retains an immediate self-sufficiency within the natural world. In both the figural and modern (or secular) attitudes toward history the importance of the earthly event is preserved: in the first instance because the historical event cannot be interpreted as a prefiguration unless it is retained for that purpose, but in the second because the event itself is of immediate and temporal sufficiency. The poetic imitation of a redeemed natural world obviously would be impossible in the figural view of reality, and in the thoroughly secular view it would be unnecessary. The view of reality relevant to this poetic interest should be thought of as non-figural, but not so completely emancipated from the divine that it is entirely secular. The reason for this is that although the events and agents of the natural world are ultimately accepted as sufficient, that world is not without the influence of the heavenly. The stages in Western literature which reveal this dissolution of the figural in the direction of the secular are traced by Auerbach in his chapters in *Mimesis* on the medieval mystery play, Dante, and Boccaccio.[10]

In the 12th and 13th century scriptural dramatizations Auerbach discovers a definite movement away from the more legendary aspects of biblical story toward the commonplaces of everyday reality. This is not surprising, he observes, because in the world of Christianity the humble and the sublime are merged.

The medieval Christian drama falls perfectly within this tradition. Being a living representation of Biblical episodes as contained, with their innately dramatic elements, in the liturgy, it opens its arms invitingly to receive the simple and untutored and to lead them from the concrete, the everyday, to the hidden and true.[11]

This combination of the humble and the sublime, the temporal and the absolute, "implies that every occurrence, in all its everyday reality, is simultaneously a part in the world-historical context through which each part is related to every other, and thus is likewise to be regarded as being of all times or above all time"

---

[10] Figural interpretation developed along with the four-fold allegorical interpretation of scripture which was needed to handle the Old Testament in Christian terms. Both figural and allegorical interpretation reflect an attitude toward reality which requires the manifest, concrete event to contain a latent meaning. But, as Auerbach points out, allegorization is quite different from figural interpretation. In allegorization the temporal is transformed into a mystical or ethical system, while figuralism retains more of the vividness of the concrete and historical. See "Figura", pp. 54-6.

[11] *Mimesis* (New York, Anchor Books, 1957), p. 135.

(*Mimesis*, p. 136). There is only a single context of history in this Christian drama, bounded on one end by the Creation and on the other by the Second Coming. And within this context there is a single action: the redemption of man. The mystery play, Auerbach comments, is a typical example of the figural representation of reality. The events of history from the Creation through the Incarnation and Passion to the Second Coming are all parts of the great drama which progresses upwards to the final apocalyptic salvation of man in God. Although the subject of the mystery play is spiritual and of the utmost sublimity, the treatment, according to Auerbach, aims to be popular:

> The ancient and sublime occurrence [the Fall] is to become immediate and present; it is to be a current event which could happen any time, which every listener can imagine and is familiar with. . . . The dialogue between Adam and Eve . . . is turned into a scene of simplest everyday reality. Sublime as it is, it becomes a scene in simple, low style. (*Mimesis*, 131)

Although the temporal event is a necessary element in figuralism, and therefore not inconsistent in these plays, the secular dimension eventually does come to dominate the figural meaning in scriptural dramatizations. The kind of conjunction of low style and sublime subject referred to in the passage quoted above is often and erroneously called, Auerbach points out, the "secularization" of Christian drama. Since the merger of the natural event and the spiritual meaning is a necessary part of figural representation, it is only accurate to speak of the secularization of scriptural drama when the natural event becomes totally separated from any ultimate meaning in the context of the Christian view of history. The medieval scriptural drama, Auerbach concludes, is thoroughly figural, although it appears that the mixture of earthly treatment and divine meaning provides fertile ground for the eventual separation of the temporal event from its heavenly goal.

In his chapter on Dante in *Mimesis*, "Farinata and Cavalcante", Auerbach argues that although the *Commedia* epitomizes medieval figuralism, it destroyed the figural world in the very process of creating it. In medieval Christian figuralism it is necessary that "historical reality is not annulled, but confirmed and fulfilled by the deeper meaning"; but Auerbach suggests that Dante, in the act of preserving the sensory, historical, and everyday reality of life, managed to annul and dissolve that deeper meaning. First of all the subject matter, like that of the mystery play, is sublime; but the style is both elevated and low. It is a poem "in which all imaginable spheres of reality appear: past and present, sublime grandeur and vile vulgarity, history and legend, tragic and comic occurrences, man and nature" (*Mimesis,* 165). The inhabitants of the *Inferno* possess a reality of the sensory experience of life, Auerbach argues; yet they remain in their respective states eternally.

Dante, then, took over earthly historicity into his beyond; his dead are cut off from the earthly present and its vicissitudes, but the memory and the most intense interest in it stirs them so profoundly that the atmosphere of the beyond is charged with it. This is less pronounced on the Mount of Purgatory and in Paradise, because there the souls do not look back upon life on earth, as they do in Hell. but forward and up; as a result, the farther we ascend the more clearly is earthly existence seen together with its divine goal. But earthly existence remains always manifest. (*Mimesis,* 168-9)

This constant manifestation of earthly existence is evidence, Auerbach observes, of Dante's concern with human action and conflict as it exists in its temporal or horizontal extension, although the vertical line to heaven, represented by the Christian drama of the Assumption, is meant to be the primary emphasis of the poem. The fulfillment of an earthly prefiguration is to be of greater importance than the temporal event itself, but Dante's interest in providing an effective poetic reality for his supernatural world results in the subordination of the divine fulfillment by the experiences of actual existence. Dante's beyond is meant to be both phenomenal and eternal, but according to Auerbach he carried the phenomenal so far that

... it breaks bounds and proclaims its independence. Figure surpasses fulfillment, or more properly: the fulfillment serves to bring out the figure in still more impressive relief. ... All through the poem there are instances in which the effect of the earthly figure and its earthly destiny surpasses or is subserved by the effect produced by its eternal situation. (*Mimesis*, 174-5)

The emotion of the reader is all too often engaged by the human conflicts rather than with "the divine order in which they have found their fulfillment". In the *Commedia*, Auerbach concludes, "the image of man eclipses the image of God. Dante's work made man's Christian-figural being a reality, and destroyed it in the very process of realizing it" (*Mimesis*, 176).

Although it hardly would be accurate to extend this thesis to claim that Dante disintegrated that attitude toward history which depends on the ultimate assumption of man by the divine (or the natural by the spiritual), Auerbach's study of Dante enables us to see that the issues and conflicts of earthly existence have become important in themselves, distinct to a certain extent from their resolution in the eternity of the divine order. It has become possible, in other words, to look forward to the poetic representation of a redemptive process which takes place fully within the world of nature rather than through an ascent to the world of spirit.

Boccaccio serves Auerbach as the next example in his exploration of this development from the figural to the secular. In the *Decamerone*, Boccaccio's characters "live on earth and only on earth". The abundance of phenomena is seen directly as a "rich world of earthly forms". In Boccaccio there is no trace "of the figural-Christian conception which pervaded Dante's imitation of the earthly and human world and which gave it power and depth" (*Mimesis*, p. 196). It is a "doctrine" of love and nature which controls the fiction of the *Decamerone*; not, as in the figural tradition, a doctrine of final assumption into the order of heaven. In his treatment of love Boccaccio is "concerned exclusively with the sensual and the real"; his heritage is the earlier idealism of love, but now "the beloved is no longer an inaccessible mistress or an incarnation of the divine idea, but the object of sexual desire" (*Mimesis*, 198).

The *Decameron* develops a distinct, thoroughly practical and secular code rooted in the right to love, an ethics which in its very essence is anti-Christian. It is presented with much grace and without any strong claim to a doctrinal validity. (*Mimesis*, 198)

It is a naturalistic ethic. The sexual impulse in man, a command of nature, is not to be resisted.

This world of Boccaccio's is a result partially, Auerbach suggests, of the vacuum left by Dante's mitigation of figural representation. With the demands of nature now distinct from an apocalyptic fulfillment in the world of spirit, the earthly and sensuous reality as it appears in the *Decamerone* lacks a "constructive ethical force". The human (and particularly the erotic) has become totally divorced from the divine in Boccaccio; and although a fully developed constructive ethical force to interpret human life has not replaced the lost divine order, there are indications in Boccaccio of the later humanistic concern with the tragic and comic implications of the conflicts of human life.

The worldliness of men like Boccaccio was still too insecure and unsupported to serve, after the fashion of Dante's figural interpretation, as a basis on which the world could be ordered, interpreted, and represented as a reality and as a whole. (*Mimesis*, 203)

With this sharp polarity established between figural and secular representations of reality (in effect between Dante and Boccaccio) I leave Auerbach's thesis. The next step is of primary importance in the discussion here, for it serves to identify, in a general way, the poetic representation of nature in the works of Spenser, Shakespeare, and Milton to be taken up in the remaining chapters. This next step is, of course, to recognize a conception of reality which although no longer figural does contain a "constructive ethical force". In the Renaissance tradition of thought and poetry which I am examining, that naturalistic ethic of Boccaccio takes its place in the corrupt lower dimension of nature. And that eternal world of divine fulfillment, which is the objective in figuralism, supplies the value of purity which takes its place in the ideal upper dimension of nature. The extreme doctrine of love and nature found in Boccaccio becomes modified by a Christian ethic, and the familiar Renaissance conflict between the perverse and the chaste use of nature enters poetry, providing the basis for a symbolic action leading to a redeemed world. This is a later literary development which represents reality as a conflict between contradictory aspects of human experience, but capable of responding to the impress of an absolute moral order for the purpose of resolving the conflict and restoring order to the natural world. Although this may appear to be a replica of the figural imitation of reality because of the presence of a higher order of ultimate values, it is in fact a severe mitigation of figuralism since the redemption of nature itself replaces the assumption of the natural by the spiritual.

Auerbach's metaphors of the vertical and horizontal line, which represent figural and secular reality, provide useful terms with which to define more clearly the characteristics of this Renaissance poetic scene. The vertical line represents a continuity of nature and spirit based on the acceptance of the temporal as well as the eternal, but in which a divine reality ultimately supercedes (or fulfills) the earthly. In the Renaissance there is a dissolution of this vertical line in the direction of the horizontal, which signifies the thoroughly temporal objectives of temporal existence. As a result of this shift from the vertical toward the horizontal, a new kind of continuity between nature and spirit is required. For poetic expression this means that a figural representation of reality is no longer possible, although the vertical connection between temporal event and its fulfillment in heaven is not so completely dissolved as to eliminate the influence of the divine upon nature. It is possible, then, to discover in Renaissance poetry a fictional world in which neither the supernatural nor the natural claims complete supremacy, although the scene of action itself is limited to the confines of the natural world. The natural asserts its claims because of the importance and acceptance of sensuous experience, and because the conflicts of human life are resolved within and not beyond the natural world itself. The supernatural asserts its claims by virtue of the rational order originating in the world of spirit which ultimately is shown to govern the world of natural experience.

That preoccupation of the age with the problem of the reconciliation of those forces which seem to pull man down in the

direction of the lower world and up in the direction of heaven
finds its dramatic expression in an imaginative scene in which
both the natural (in the form of sexual passion) and the supernatural (in the form of purity) are manifest. Those eternal worlds
of the demonic and the divine become part of temporal reality.
Instead of journeys to paradise or the inferno we find redemption
and damnation completed within the natural world. The theme
of the redemption of nature, or the realignment of the natural
with the spiritual, is an attempt in literary art to present a vision
of a perfected natural world in which a harmony is established
between the lowest level of the sensuous (which borders on the
world of hell) and the highest level of the pure (which borders
on the world of heaven). Such an objective as this, which depends
on a subtle balance of natural and spiritual demands, requires
the creation of a fictional world of corresponding formal subtlety
in order that the entire range of two-dimensional nature, from
the point where it is linked to hell to the point where it is linked
to heaven, may be represented.

B. EMBELLISHED NATURE

Conceptions of imitation and decorum in Renaissance criticism,
both Italian and English, are treated in this section in order to
demonstrate that there is a theoretical foundation in the 16th and
17th century version of poetic theory for the previous assertion
that much of the poetry of the age represents a more pronounced
temporal reality without totally relinquishing the expression of
those forces which exist beyond nature, and that one of the most
significant forms which this shift in world-view takes is the theme
of the redemption or perfection of nature.

An essential element in that world view is belief in the potential of man and nature to achieve perfection. The prevailing
attitude in this tradition is that grace does not destroy nature but
perfects it. The same attitude is transferred to that body of ideas
commonly designated as Renaissance poetics, and becomes the
proclamation that "art perfects nature". Just as an ideal natural

order is projected in Hooker's image of the world of grace (*lex aeterna*) revealing itself in the world of nature in the form of natural law, so the creation of a similar natural order is indicated by the critics to be the function of art. The directive, "follow nature", can mean, therefore, to imitate an ideal nature and by so doing improve upon a disordered nature – the poetic counterpart to the idea of the perfection of nature by grace. It is this conception of imitation in poetry which is relevant to the argument here.[12]

For Sidney, the poet may range "into the divine consideration of what may be and should be". He "dooth growe in effect another nature, in making things either better than Nature bringeth forth, or, quite a newe . . .". The world of nature is brazen, that of the poets golden. And unlike the historian who is "bound to tell things as things were", the poet can "be liberall of a perfect patterne".[13] In addition to the concept of imitation which consists of the belief that poetry is able to exceed nature, the distinction made by Sidney between history and poetry is significant. The writing of history is an unselected process because of the requirement that events be recorded as they were. History "follows nature" in the sense that an unpatterned stream of happenings is set down. Poetry "follows nature" in the sense that the ideal form of experience is imitated. The historical world itself, then, is the disorder of human existence, and, as such, is a term in Renaissance criticism corresponding to that larger Renaissance concept of nature viewed as the totally fallen world and characterized by moral and physical discord. In criticism, poetry is set against history as that ideal world which gives order to the disorder of historical events. In the larger Renaissance conception,

---

[12]   Imitation, in Renaissance criticism, is also used to mean the Aristotelian imitation of an action, or broadened to mean the imitation of objects, the passions, truth, and knowledge, or to mean the imitation of the manner and content of great classical and vernacular authors. The concept is limited here to the imitation of nature, or a more perfect rational and moral order. See Harold W. Wilson, "Some Meanings of Nature in Renaissance Literary Theory", *Journal of the History of Ideas*, II (1941), 430-48.

[13]   *An Apology for Poetry, Elizabethan Critical Essays*, ed. G. G. Smith (London, 1904), Vol. I, pp. 159, 156, 168.

grace is set against nature as the divine pattern which gives order to nature, corresponding to "poetry". Consequently, it is evident that Renaissance criticism was able to define an objective of poetic imitation which was consistent with that ideal of a perfected nature which prevailed in the larger intellectual tradition of the age.

Bacon makes a more explicit connection between the conceptions of world-view and poetic imitation:

For as the sensible world is inferior in dignity to the rational soul, Poesy seems to bestow upon human nature those things which history denies to it, and to satisfy the mind with the shadows of things when the substance cannot be obtained. For if the matter be attentively considered, a sound argument may be drawn from Poesy to show that there is agreeable to the spirit of man a more ample greatness, a more perfect order, and a more beautiful variety than it can anywhere (since the Fall) find in nature .... it may be fairly thought to partake somewhat of a divine nature, because it raises the mind and carries it aloft, accommodating the shows of things to the desires of the mind, not (like reason and history) buckling and bowing down the mind to the nature of things.[14]

The emphasis in this passage is on the effect of poetry rather than on the characteristics of the world which is imitated, but it is quite evident that for Bacon, a correspondence exists between poetry's function to carry man away from the sensible and toward the divine, and the poetic scene which accomplishes such an end. An examination of the art of poetry shows that there is an "agreement" between the "more perfect order" of the poetic world and the desire of man to rise toward the divine. There is, in other words, an intimate relationship between the imitation ("the shows of things") and "the desires of the mind". Poetry improves upon history, but it also improves man. This connection between the ends of poetry and the nature of its imitated world is widespread in Renaissance criticism. There is a tendency to speak, without clear discrimination, of poetry both as a kind of redemption (in terms of its effect on man) and as a fictional structure conveying an image of embellished or perfected nature (in terms of what is imitated). This connection, in spite of the

[14] *De dignitate et augmentis scientiarum,* in *Essays,* ed. R. F. Jones, p. 391.

ambiguity which surrounds it, seems to be a logical result of that great Renaissance objective to perfect nature and to create a poetic image of that perfected world. The goal of man and of poetry are thought to be identical.

Puttenham's *Arte of English Poesie* is the most elaborate attempt, in England, to assert a correspondence between what is to be imitated in poetry in order to achieve its good effect, and how that content is to be formally presented. Unfortunately, Puttenham does not define with much precision the nature of that content or what its structural elements are. He merely asserts that there should be a consistency between what is meant and how it is expressed. Such an assertion is a simple appeal to the familiar standard of decorum between theme and form, without indicating the exact nature of that decorous relationship.

For Puttenham just as there is a "decencie" to the art of life there is a "decencie" to the art of poetry. The entire *Arte* is characterized by continual recourse to such terms as good conformitie, just correspondencie, convenient proportion, decencie, comelynesse, seemelynesse, concord, congruity, and decorum. These terms apply to the manner in which man conducts himself as well as to the way in which the art of poetry is properly accomplished. Not only does Puttenham argue for a correspondence between a "good conformitie" in life and poetry, but also for a proper proportion within the poetic work itself between theme and form. In other words, an orderly pattern should prevail in both the actual and the fictional worlds. Puttenham himself recognizes the necessity for defining this orderly pattern or "good grace":

But herin resteth the difficultie, to know what t.. good grace is, and wherein it consisteth, for peradventure it be easier to conceave than to expresse. We will therefore examin it to the bottome, and say that every thing which pleseth the mind or sences, and the mind by the sences as by means instrumentall, doth it for some amiable point or qualitie that is in it, which draweth them to a good liking and contentment with their proper objects. But that cannot be if they discover any illfavorednesse or disproportion to the partes apprehensive . . .[15]

Instead of getting to the bottom of the problem, Puttenham

[15] *Elizabethan Critical Essays*, Vol. 2, p. 173.

proceeds in a circle. He concludes that good grace is good, and
will lose its goodness with the introduction of any kind of disproportion. That is, the indecorous violates the decorous. In spite
of Puttenham's failure to define the nature of this orderly pattern
in either life or poetry, it is possible to derive its general characteristics from the implications of certain statements. First of
all, those terms of fitness and concord which govern the argument
of the *Arte* are obviously charged with moral importance. The
"good conformitie" as a pattern of life is an ethical ideal; it as-
sumes a congruity between man and some rational and virtuous
order. By employing Puttenham's own extension of this concord
into the world of art, it is possible to conclude that a moral order
should inform the fictional as well as the actual world. In much
the same way as Sidney and Bacon, Puttenham outlines a program
for art in which poetry is seen to be an imitation of a world in
which an ideal moral order prevails. In addition, he indicates
that the formal elements of that world must be consistent with
the meaning it carries.

Puttenham's statements on the relationship between art and
nature provide further evidence for the assertion that in Renaissance poetics the objective for poetry is the establishment of a
moral order. The same kind of idealism concerning the capacity
of poetic art to present a more perfectly ordered world which is
found in Sidney and Bacon is also evident in Puttenham:

In some cases we say arte is an ayde and coadjutor to nature, and a
furtherer of her actions to good effect, or peradventure a meane to
supply her wants, by renforcing the causes wherein shee is impotent
and defective .... In another respect arte is not only an aide and
coadjutor to natur. in all her actions but an alterer of them, and in
some sort a surmounter of her skill, so as by meanes of it her owne
effects shall appeare more beautiful or straunge or miraculous ....
Finally in another respect arte is, as it were, an encounterer and contrary to nature, producing effects neither like to hers, nor by participation with her operations, nor by imitation of her patternes, but
makes things and produceth effects altogether straunge and diverse,
of such forme & qualitie (nature alwaies supplying stuffe) as she never
would or could have done of her self.[16]

[16] *Ibid.,* Vol. 2, pp. 187, 188, 189.

Whether art is conceived of as supplying what nature lacks, surmounting nature, or contrary to nature, it is clear that Puttenham means to indicate that the fictional world can represent a more perfect nature, for his observations are limited to the difference between the actual historical nature and what poetry can do to embellish rather than transcend that nature. The Renaissance critics often speak of the relationship between nature and art in terms of a defective and reformed nature, between the sensible and the rational, the brazen and the golden, what is and what ought to be. When such properties of embellishment as the rational, the golden, and what ought to be are limited to the natural world itself rather than extended to a transcendent order of perfection, it is clear that there is a theoretical foundation in Renaissance poetics for the imitation of a restored natural world. That ideal of order with which the age was preoccupied has its correspondence in the metaphor of the golden world of poetic imitation.

Such a conclusion points up the insufficiency of the common explanation for the idealism of the Renaissance critics, who are said to be apologists primarily interested in improving the reputation of the art of poetry. Identifying the imitated world with a perfected nature, opposing poetry to history, and arguing that "feigning" is a form of truth certainly cannot be accounted for completely by the familiar explanation that the most important objective in Renaissance poetics is the defense of poetry as a respectable branch of "learning". Rather, each one of these emphases reflects a tendency to relate poetry's ability to embellish nature symbolically to that pervasive Renaissance belief in the capacity of nature to be embellished morally.

This tendency is most clearly evident in the parallelism of the statements "grace perfects nature" and "art perfects nature". However, because of the confusion created by that ambiguous attitude which on one hand viewed art as redemptive itself and on the other viewed art as the imitation of a redeemed condition and because of the concept of imitation involved, it is now more accurate to say that while grace perfects nature, art imitates a perfected nature. Such a formula for art is still insufficient because it is impossible to believe that every literary work will represent a perfect natural order. Not only does simple observation of Renaissance literature deny this; it is aso inconsistent with that tradition of thought outlined in the first chapter. According to that view of the world, fallen man exists in a fallen world in a mediate position, capable of aligning himself either with the values of the world of spirit as they inform the upper dimension of nature, or with the values of the brutish aspects of the lower dimension of nature. The desired upward alignment is of course the result of a struggle between the two contradictory aspects of experience. Conflict, in other words, is a necessary element in the content of this world view; it is a conflict ultimately resolved by the realignment of the natural with the spiritual. For this reason, it appears that the Renaissance critics, in making a simple equation between the imitated world and a perfected nature, have ignored that "dramatic tension of responsibility" which is an essential part of the theme of the redemption of nature.

Such a conclusion, however, is not valid when one considers that the ultimate objective is the same whether in criticism the fictional world is said to present a gilded nature, or whether the poetry which is concerned with this issue presents a conflict which is finally resolved in the total concord of a gilded nature. In addition, in most of the statements concerning the imitation of nature already quoted, there is no indication that the poet must immediately and dogmatically represent a redeemed nature. If poetry shows "the causes wherein shee is impotent and defective," there is implied that process by which potency and the removal of defect are achieved. The formula for art, in other words, should be altered to read: poetry imitates that process toward perfection as well as perfected nature itself.

In this connection, M. H. Abrams claims that the Renaissance has a "pragmatic theory" of art, a theory which "looks at the work of art chiefly as a means to an end". He opposes the pragmatic theory to the later "objective theory" which sees a poem as "a world of its own, independent of the world into which we are born". He asserts that the "central tendency of the pragmatic critic is to conceive a poem as something made in order to effect requisite responses in its readers", while the later theory saw a poem as a "heterocosm" or a second nature, subject only to its own laws.[17] It must be recognized, however, that in the Renaissance concept of imitation there is indeed a provision for the creation of a "second nature" (more perfect than the first), and that the fictional world is viewed as not only having a redemptive effect on the reader, but as figuring forth the redemption or improvement of the world. In accounting for Renaissance criticism, then, emphasis should be placed equally on the content of that "second nature" which is imitated, and on the effect that imitation is meant to have on the reader. The ideal form of poetry is both heuristic and symbolically independent.

According to conclusions already reached, the theme of the redemption of nature involves a conflict between the forces of the two levels of nature resulting finally in the establishment of a harmony between the double demands (limited here to passion and purity). If the formal elements of the imitated world are to be consistent with this thematic balance between the content of the natural world and the impress of the supernatural world (which includes both the divine and the demonic), it is necessary that the imitated world be nature itself, but a nature which is congenial to the forces of heaven and hell. The Renaissance concept of poetic decorum provides some foundation for this imitation of a natural world which yet reveals the workings of the absolute worlds of the demonic and the divine.

The desire that the temporal world be cleansed of its demonic forces, that man move in the direction of the divine, but without relinquishing the natural world, is an essentially secular view of the world. It is reflected in the decline of the figural view of reality in which the temporal is subordinate to its fulfillment beyond nature; or in the commonplace that in the Renaissance the image of man replaces the image of God. However, in the view of the world involved here it is implicit that even though the natural world is sufficient ground for the resolution of the

[17] *The Mirror and the Lamp* (New York, Norton Library, 1958), pp. 15, 27.

conflicts of life, before there can be *concordia mundi* some manner
of contact with the universal order of the divine must be established. The influence of this mitigated figural view of reality is
evident in the Renaissance concept of poetic decorum, for the
balance between what is natural and what is unnatural governs
some aspects of this doctrine.[18]

Puttenham, in a statement already quoted, conceives of art as
aiding, altering, and opposing nature. This triple view may be
taken as the basis for the present discussion. When art aids
nature, literal reality submits to certain additions to what is
already there (a "furtherer of her actions to good effect"). When
art alters nature, literal reality is surmounted in certain ways.
And when art opposes or is "contrary to nature", literal reality
is transcended by "effects altogether straunge and diverse". For
this latter "violation" of reality, Puttenham adds the significant
qualification that the "forme and qualitie" of this strangeness is
supplied by the "stuffe" of nature. There is, then, in each of
these relationships between art and literal reality, including the
most extreme separation, a refusal to allow the possibility of
imitating a world totally disconnected from the stuff of nature,
or totally supernatural. The "contrary to nature" conception,
however, suggests that the stuff of nature is balanced by effects
"as she never would or could have done of her selfe". The two
extremities of Puttenham's triple concept provide a foundation
for a doctrine of decorum. The *aiding* of nature in poetry places
the fictional world a relatively short distance from literal reality,
while the *opposition* to nature in poetry places the fictional world
the furthest distance from this reality which can be allowed without breaking the desired link with the stuff of nature. A just
proportion between that which is natural and empirically credible,
and that which is "altogether straunge and diverse" constitutes
that aspect of decorum which provides for a balance between the
imitation of the natural and the supernatural.

Bacon writes in *The Advancement of Learning* that the poetic

---

[18]   Decorum is a most comprehensive doctrine in Renaissance criticism,
including character and action, style, poetic justice, genre, etc. The concept is limited here to the decorum of the credible imitation.

imagination, not being tied to the laws of matter, "may at pleasure joyne that which Nature hath severed, & sever that which Nature hath joyned, and so make unlawful Matches and divorces of things".[19] According to the doctrine of decorum involved here, such violations of literal reality must be tempered so that the world of nature does not cease to be the basic scene of the poetic imitation. It is the Italian rather than the English critics who concern themselves with the particulars of this decorum. In their treatment of the "decorum of a credible imitation", these critics deal with the verisimilar, the probable, the credible, and the marvelous as significant parts of the larger principle.

Tasso, in grappling with the problem of the relationship between the true and the marvelous, demonstrates that the marvelous is a necessary dimension of poetry and is not antithetical to the true:

The natures of these two things, the marvelous and the lifelike, are very different, and different in such a way that they are like contraries, yet both of them are necessary in a poem, though the art of an excellent poet is required to couple them .... I hold that the same action can be both marvelous and true. ... Some actions which greatly exceed the power of men the poet attributes to God, his angels, to devils, or to those whom God or the devils have conceded this power, such as the saints, magicians, and fairies. These actions, if they are considered of themselves, appear marvelous .... If one regards the virtue and power of the doer, these same things will be judged true to life, because ... God and his ministers, and by his permission the demons and magicians, are able to do wondrous, things exceeding the force of nature .... The same action, then, can be both marvelous and according to verisimilitude, marvelous when thought of for itself and circumscribed within the limits of nature, true to life when considered apart from those limits and with respect to its cause, which is a force, supernatural, powerful, and accustomed to bring about similar marvels.[20]

The marvelous exceeds the force of nature, but both the marvelous and the life-like are a form of truth and are admissible in

---

[19] *Critical Essays of the Seventeenth Century,* ed. Joel E. Spingarn (Oxford, 1908), Vol. I, p. 5.
[20] "Discourses on the Heroic Poem", *Literary Criticism: Plato to Dryden,* ed. Allan H. Gilbert (New York, 1940), pp. 480-81.

poetic imitation. From this assertion it is clear that the false has been removed as an element of poetic imitation, but Tasso recognizes that it is necessary to employ the marvelous with caution:

> But [the poet] should not be too free in feigning things that are impossible, monstrous, supernatural, and unfitting .... The author should consider the power of the magic art and of nature itself, as though inclosed within certain limits and confined by certain laws. (Gilbert, 489-90)

The recourse to "nature itself" and "certain laws" suggests that Tasso is invoking what might be called the poetic counterpart to the law of nature in order to control the imitation of both the supernatural and the natural within poetry.

For Mazzoni, the poetic imitation must fulfill a standard of credibility, a standard which allows, however, the representation of both the sensible and the supersensible worlds:

> ... since the poet always has to do with the credible, he should of necessity treat all things in a manner suited to the credible, that is, he should always avail himself of individual and perceptible means in representing the things of which he speaks, whatever they are. Therefore when he treats things pertaining to contemplative teaching he should make every effort to represent them with sensible images .... But in this Dante is certainly marvelous .... From this we can conclude it is not forbidden to the poet to treat things pertaining to the sciences and to the speculative intellect, if only he treats them in a credible manner, making idols and poetic images, as Dante surely has done with marvelous and noble artifice, in representing with idols and beautiful images before the eyes of everyone all intellectual being and the intelligible world itself. I remember that Plato in the *Phaedrus*, exalting his invention, wrote as follows: "But the place that is above the heavens no one of the poets ever has treated or even will treat as it should be done". ... But if he had seen the third *Cantica* of Dante he would without any doubt have ... given the palm to Dante and consequently to the poets for knowing how to make idols and images fitted for making the people understand the quality of the super-celestial world. (Gilbert, 365-6)

He concludes that "the credible as marvelous is the subject of poetry, for the poet should utter not merely credible things but marvelous things as well". The poet may falsify human and natural history and go on to "impossible things" as long as the representation remains credible. Poetry, finally, is "an imitation, made with harmony, with rhythm, and with verse, accompanied or joined with matter that is credible and marvelous" (Gilbert, 370, 372).

Both the sensible and the supersensible worlds may be represented in poetry as long as a standard of credibility is maintained. Such a standard reflects the need to retain the life-like or the natural, but at the same time to allow the marvelous or the supernatural. It is a requirement that corresponds to Puttenham's assertion that the imitated world may be contrary to nature but not relinquish the stuff of nature. When this provision in Renaissance poetic theory which allows for the imitation of both the natural and the supernatural is combined with the former provision that poetry can imitate the perfection of nature, it becomes evident that there is a broad theoretical base in the Renaissance concept of art for the poetic theme of the redemption of nature. In the Renaissance concept of imitation traced here a fictional world consisting of an embellished or perfected nature is claimed for poetry. And in the concept of a balanced or decorous relationship between the imitation of the sensible and the supersensible a fictional world consisting essentially of images of the natural, but open to images of the supernatural is claimed. The thematic interest, then, finds its formal provisions in these aspects of Renaissance poetics.

C. THE ROMANTIC MODE

The attitudes toward man and nature with which I have been dealing quite clearly substantiate an observation such as Auerbach's concerning the dissolution of a vertical or figural interpretation of the destiny of man in favor of a more secular attitude which maintained that, with certain qualifications, the range of the natural world was sufficient ground for the fulfillment of the potential of man. The effects of such a shift in attitude are of course apparent in the representation of reality in art. I have suggested that this concentration of interest in the Renaissance on the renewal and restoration of the best elements which reside potentially in man and nature is conveyed in literature through the theme of the redemption of nature. In addition, the formal elements of the poetic expression of this theme are designed to imitate a world which is restricted to the range of nature but includes a representation of super-natural influences.

The three poems of Spenser, Shakespeare, and Milton reveal this theme and the formal structure that is correlative to it. These works are concerned with chaste heroines and the conflict of passion and purity which is within or around them. Such a conflict and its resolution, as I have pointed out, may be taken as a representation of the conflict between the two dimensions of nature and their reconciliation, which constitutes the perfection of nature. In addition, I want to suggest, before examining the works themselves, that there is in all the works a generally common mode of imitation consisting of an action which opposes innocence and experience, and a scene which is limited to the range of nature but includes images of heaven and hell. In order to identify this mode more precisely I will employ what Northrop Frye, in *Anatomy of Criticism*, defines as the "romantic mode", for in this form of imitation the values of innocence are cherished, the narrative moves within the cyclical or mutable world of nature, but with indications of vertical movements in the direction of the upper or lower worlds, and the aim of the fiction is commonly a goal of reconciliation and integration.

In order to locate that mode which Frye calls romantic within the context of his whole scheme of fictional modes, a brief description of that scheme is necessary. Five general fictional forms are distinguished from each other in terms of the different relationships which exist between the hero and his external world. The first is the mythic mode, in which the hero is a god; or in other terms, the hero and his world are distinctly superior in kind to the mortal and his world. In the second or romantic mode, the hero and his world are superior in degree but not in kind to other men, and there is a tendency to suspend the ordinary laws of nature to allow the hero to perform acts uncommon to ordinary man. The third mode, the high mimetic, presents a hero who is superior in degree to other men, but similar in environment. He is commonly a leader; and his actions are subject as other men's to social forces and the laws of nature. The high mimetic hero is most often the hero of tragedy. In the fourth or low mimetic mode, the hero is exactly like other men in degree and environment. The same "canons of probability" pertain for him as for us. He is the hero found in comedy or realistic fiction. The last mode, the ironic, portrays a hero inferior in power and intelligence to other men. In his experiences we feel we are observing a scene of bondage, frustration, or absurdity. Frye asserts that these modes should be thought of as a circular progression, with the ironic mode revealing a return to the original mythic mode. Each successive relationship between the hero and the world is progressively more removed from the expression of that hero and world as supernatural, until finally in the ironic mode the life of the "hero" becomes a bitter parody of the mythic ideal of man divine in a divine or supernatural world.[21]

In addition to the movement of character away from the god-like and supernatural, the fictional modes reveal a movement toward a scene which more and more exactly represents the characteristics of empirical reality. The physical laws of nature and the canons of natural probability become increasingly more evident. This transformation of character, action, and setting is termed displacement. In describing that displacement which occurs between the mythic and the romantic fictional modes, Frye writes:

The central principle of displacement is that what can be metaphorically identified in a myth can only be linked in romance by some form of simile, analogy, significant association, incidental accompanying imagery, and the like . . . . First, there is the undisplaced myth, generally concerned with gods or demons . . . . Second we have the general tendency we have called romantic, the tendency to suggest implicit mythical patterns in a world more closely associated with human experience. (*Anatomy*, pp. 137-40)

Romance, in other words, reveals the displacement of myth in the direction of actual human life, but yet does not move fully

[21] See "Historical Criticism: Theory of Modes", *Anatomy of Criticism* (Princeton, 1957), pp. 33-52.

into that area of realism (the realm of the high and low mimetic modes). In its medial position, then, romance retains some of the characteristics of the supernatural world of myth, but is enough removed from this mode so that its content may be associated with the experiences of the natural world. The fictional world of romance, as so far described, can be related to some earlier conclusions. It is apparent that some connection can be made between the displacement of the mythic world in the direction of the romantic, and the dissolution of the vertical line of figuralism in the direction of the horizontal line of secularism. The romantic fictional mode is located between modes of essentially supernatural representation on one hand and essentially natural on the other. It partakes of both, but is more definitely an imitation of a natural world which contains actions, images, and forms of analogy attesting to the presence of either gods or demons within nature. In the same way, that mitigation of figural reality, which I have identified previously, reveals the rejection of a supernatural resolution to a human action or event, and accepts the sufficiency of the natural world, but not so entirely that the impress of both the divine and demonic worlds upon nature is not recognized. It is clear that both the romantic mode, as so far described, and the shift from a figural representation of reality toward the secular provide for a poetic structure limited to a natural world, but a natural world which reveals the presence of demons and gods, the demonic and the divine, hell and heaven.

Frye also describes, in the *Anatomy*, two fundamental narrative patterns, the cyclical and the dialectic. They both govern the action in the romantic mode; the first directly, the second in a more restricted way. The cyclical movement of narrative is described as taking place fully within the natural order, and is intimately associated with the mutable, evolving patterns of nature. It is the basic narrative movement of those modes which are displaced from the supernatural world of the mythic mode. The two poles of this cycle of action (that is, the top and bottom of the circle) are called by Frye the world of innocence (at the top) and the world of experience (at the bottom). The comic action proceeds from experience to innocence, the tragic from

innocence to experience. In an ironic narrative the world of experience prevails, and in a romantic narrative the world of innocence prevails. The romantic plot involves an ideal innocent
world which may be threatened by the world of experience, but
in which innocence ultimately is victorious.

Beyond the cycle of nature there are two realms, in Frye's
classifications, which are eternally unchanging, and which represent the two poles between which the dialectic narrative action
takes place. One pole is called the apocalyptic (corresponding to
heaven or the divine world). It is located outside the limits of
nature, but in close proximity to that world of innocence at the
peak of the cycle of nature. The other pole is called the demonic
(corresponding to hell). It is also located outside the limits of
nature, but in close proximity to that world of experience in the
depths of nature. Those points at which the eternal worlds of the
divine and the demonic come into contact with those two dimensions of nature – innocence and experience – are called by Frye,
speaking in terms of poetic imitation, epiphanies.[22] Actions involving a transfer from the natural world to one of these eternal
regions constitutes the dialectic narrative pattern. Familiar examples are the process of Christian salvation by which man passes
from earth to heaven, and the process of damnation by which
man passes from earth to hell. The apocalyptic dialectic narrative
pattern can be exemplified most clearly, of course, by the Christ
narrative in which the ordeal of the Passion is followed by resurrection and assumption into the divine world. The literature
dealing with the Christian pilgrim (particularly the moral allegory

[22] Concerning these epiphanies, Frye writes in a later essay that there
are "two points of particular significance in poetic symbolism. One is the
point, usually the top of a mountain just below the moon, where the upper
world and this one come into alignment, where we look up to the heavenly
world and down on the turning cycle of nature. The other is the point,
usually in a mysterious labyrinthine cave, where the lower world and this
one come into alignment, where we look down to a world of pain and up
to the turning cycle of nature. This upward perspective sees the same
world, though from the opposite pole, as the downward perspective in the
vision of ascent, and hence the same cyclical symbols may be employed
for it" ("New Directions from Old", *Myth and Mythmaking,* ed. Henry A.
Murray [New York, 1960], p. 123). See also, *Anatomy,* pp. 131-206.

of the Middle Ages) presents a comparable pattern in which the pilgrim undergoes trials and ordeals within the world of nature before his assumption into the apocalyptic world.

Since the romantic mode has as its location the world of nature, we would not expect a dialectic action removing man from nature, either to heaven or to hell, to be present. However, those two aspects of nature – innocence and experience – are intimately associated with the regions of the divine and the demonic, and are in fact natural counterparts to them. The value of innocence has as its source the purity of the divine or apocalyptic world, and the corruptions of experience have their source in the regions of hell or the demonic. Thus there is an implied dialectic relationship between innocence and the divine, and between experience and the demonic, although the romantic narrative itself takes place within the natural world. The romantic narrative does not present a pattern of death, resurrection, and assumption into the divine world after an ordeal within nature, but rather its "natural" or displaced counterpart of figurative death and restoration within nature after a similar temporal ordeal. The *vita nuova* into which Dante enters (in the work of that title) is apocalyptic to all appearances, yet the entry occurs within the order of this life (nature), and, as such, this regeneration differs from the entry into the truly divine world identified at the end of the *Paradiso*.

The romantic mode, then, reveals a pattern of action which takes place within the world of nature, but has a figurative dialectic relationship with the eternal worlds of the divine and the demonic.

It is clear that Frye's conception of a dialectic narrative action and Auerbach's conception of a figural representation of reality are identical. They both provide for the dramatization of an event or a series of events which reaches its completion only in a region beyond nature. The cyclical narrative action, on the other hand, in which conflict arises and is resolved within the natural world, corresponds to Auerbach's conception of the secular representation of reality. The romantic mode, in addition, presents an action limited to the world of nature, yet reveals the presence of the supernatural in that world, and thus corresponds to that Renaissance attitude which accepts the sufficiency of the natural only when it is informed by a divine order.

In pointing out these links between Frye's description of a romantic poetic scene and action, and those Renaissance attitudes toward reality previously outlined, it is possible to add the correspondence which exists between innocence and experience, and purity and passion. Innocence and experience provide the two dimensions of the cyclical world of nature in the romantic mode. Innocence is associated with the divine world, and experience with the demonic. And one of the objectives of the action of the romantic mode is to assure the primacy of innocence in its conflict with the world of experience. Similarly, passion and purity exemplify the two aspects of that divided nature which form an important part of the Renaissance world view. Passion, or the sensual level of nature, imbrutes man; its power is associated with the corruptions of the world of hell. Purity, or the rational level of nature, raises man in the direction of the angels; its power is associated with the world of the divine. The scheme which Frye defines for the romantic mode of poetic imitation corresponds to the Renaissance image of a four-fold universe, for in both instances heaven and hell surround a two-level nature. In addition, both constructions include a conflict between these levels, and indicate that the objective is the rejection of the powers of hell and the recognition of the powers of heaven, an objective to be gained without removing man from nature and renouncing the forces of life.

III. SPENSER

A. LOVE, MARRIAGE, AND THE "EPITHALAMION"

In the poems of Spenser, Shakespeare, and Milton to be treated in these chapters, the conflict between Venus and Diana, and its resolution, take shape in a metaphorical world in which the cyclical world of human experience is not transcended in favor of the eternal world of the divine; yet it retains the influence of that divine world and, temporarily, of the demonic world. Between the extremes of heaven and hell, the natural world exists as fallen or corrupt, with the potential of being pulled down in the direction of sin, corruption and death, or raised in the direction of the purity and order of the divine. The figure of man as *compositum mixtum*, part beast and part angel, stands at the center of this fallen world, capable of restoring himself and his world, or of imbruting himself by submission to the forces of the demonic.

In this tradition of thought, and in the poetry which dramatizes these ideas, the concern is with the redemption rather than the renunciation of nature; therefore, the dialectic movement of man out of nature to heaven is replaced by a cyclical movement within nature away from the corrupt and chaotic and toward purity and rational order, away from the brutish and toward the angelic, away from lust and toward true love. The older figural representation of man's fulfillment in a supernatural paradise is replaced by a more secular representation of man's fulfillment in an earthly paradise, or a perfected nature.

The disjuncture of nature and spirit is the basic identity of such a view of the universe, but in the world of human experience the discord takes the form of the conflict between sensuality and reason, or, for my purposes here, between sexual passion and bodily purity. In the poetic theme of the redemption of nature this tension between the demands of Venus and Diana is dramatized and resolved. The reason for concentrating on these particular contradictory aspects of experience is that sexual passion and absolute chastity identify the conflicting forces of the two levels of nature, and that their reconciliation represents the perfection or redemption of nature. Absolute chastity is the natural and human counterpart to the eternal purity of the divine order; and sexual passion is the natural and human counterpart to the sin and corruption of the demonic order. The reconciliation of these opposites tempers wanton sexuality with the quality of chastity, but it does not amount to a rejection of fleshly desire or "natural felicity" in favor of eternal virginity.

Each of the main works to be discussed in the following chapters presents a fictional world in which the demonic, the natural, and the divine exist in that particular kind of equilibrium already indicated as a requirement for the imitation of a redeemed but not transcended nature. The chaste love heroine is the central character of these works. She not only has her own destiny to fulfill by reconciling the forces of Venus and Diana within her, but she serves to crystalize and give meaning to the complexity of forces and characters which contribute to the expression of the theme. The chaste love heroine contains within her the capacity not only to solve her own problems but to form the bond between nature and spirit and thus redeem the fictional world of nature. That is, her purity aligns her with the upper world, and her desire for love introduces the baser aspects of the natural world. The solution to this problem of purity vs. passion in terms of "chaste desire" or "true love" is a harmonious compromise which represents the redemption of the natural world of the poem, for the lower level of nature (sexual desire) is cleansed but not obliterated by the upper level (chastity).

The primary contention in the discussion of all these poems is that the conflict of sexuality and chastity, and the subsequent equilibrium between them, is an extensive and complex metaphor for the large issue of the tension which prevails between a fallen and divine world, and for the perfection of the natural order which is meant to dissolve this tension. With the quality of chastity the most "divine" and the quality of sexuality the most "natural", the problems of human love are able to carry this heavier burden of meaning in Renaissance poetry. It is not too much to expect that all the elements surrounding a drama of "chaste love" have been designed to imitate a perfected or embellished world, and not simply to tell us poetically that true love is something like salvation. Redemption of man or the restoration of his world do not function in these poems as rhetorical support for the virtuous condition of true love; rather, the virtuous condition of true love functions as a complex metaphor for the restoration of man and his fallen world.

This metaphor of love is more complex in Spenser than in Shakespeare or Milton in the sense that love, for Spenser, can create a cosmic perfection extending to the limits of the created universe, but it can also bring about the disintegration of man, and nature with him. Love may create discord or concord, depending on whether it is wanton or chaste.

> ... if you loosely love without respect,
> It is no love, but a discordant warre,
> Whose unlike parts amongst themselves do jarre.
>
> For love is a celestiall harmonie,
> Of likely harts composed of starres concent.[1]

The association of love with harmony and order is a most important principle in the poetry of Spenser; it will become clear eventually that this association is the basis for an elaborate metaphorical device designed to represent that great goal of the Renaissance mind – *concordia mundi*.

Such a goal of order is often identified in the Renaissance with what might be called the "double eschatology" of the metaphor

---

[1] "An Hymne in Honour of Beautie", ll. 194-98, *The Poetical Works,* eds. J. C. Smith and E. De Selincourt (London, 1912).

of the Golden Age. This ideal is a condition of purity and order
which existed before the fall of man and his world, but it is also
a condition projected into the future and equated with the perfection of man and all nature. Spenser interrupts his narrative in
the fourth book of *The Faerie Queene* to present his conception
of this lost but restorable age, and the nature of its decay:

> But antique age, yet in the infancie
> Of time, did live then like an innocent,
> In simple truth and blamelesse chastitie,
> Ne then of guile had made experiment;
> But, void of vile and treacherous intent,
> Held virtue for it selfe in soveraine awe:
> Then loyall love had royall regiment,
> And each unto his lust did make a lawe,
> From all forbidden things his liking to withdraw.
>
> The Lyon there did with the Lambe consort,
> And eke the Dove sate by the Faulcons side;
> Ne each of other feared fraud or tort,
> And did in safe securitie abide,
> Withouten perill of the stronger pride:
> But when the world woxe old, it woxe warre old,
> (Whereof it hight) and, having shortly tride
> The traines of wit, in wickenesse woxe bold,
> And dared of all sinnes the secrets to unfold.
>
> Then beautie, which was made to represent
> The great Creatours owne resemblance bright,
> Unto abuse of lawlesse lust was lent,
> And made the baite of bestiall delight:
> Then faire grew foule, and foule grew faire in sight;
> And that, which wont to vanquish God and man,
> Was made a vassal of the victors might;
> Then did her glorious flowre wex dead and wan,
> Despisd and troden downe of all that over-ran.
>
> And now it is so utterly decayd,
> That any bud thereof doth scarse remaine,
> But-if few plants, preserv'd through heavenly ayd,
> In Princes Court doe hap to sprout agame,
> Dew'd with her drops of bountie soveraine,
> Which from that goodly glorious flowre proceed,
> Sprung of the auncient stocke of Princes straine,

> Now th'onely remnant of that royall breed,
> Whose noble kind at first was sure of heavenly seed.
>
> (4.8.30-33)

The debilitating effects of human passion described in this passage are emphasized throughout Spenser's poetry, and collectively take on the larger meaning of the moral decay of man and the complementary decay of the elemental world around him. In "An Hymne of Love", Spenser writes:

> ... thou tyrant Love doest laught and scorne
> At their complaints, making their paine thy play;
> Whylest they lye languishing like thrals forlorne,
> The whyles thou doest triumph in their decay.
>
> (134-37)

And in the *Amoretti*, the equation of love and eternal bliss is countered in Sonnet LIII by the equation of love and death:

> Right so my cruell fayre with me doth play,
>   for with the goodly semblant of her hew
>   she doth allure me to mine owne decay,
>   and then no mercy will unto me shew.

And in Sonnet VII the double equation is most succinctly expressed:

> Fayre eyes, the myrrour of my mazed hart,
>   what wondrous vertue is contayned in you,
>   the which both lyfe and death forth from you dart
>   into the object of your mighty view?

In *The Shepheardes Calender*, too, Spenser is concerned with the disintegration of the world which results from human passion. Colin's condition of incipient fulfillment of his passion for Rosalind is one of the main dramatic concerns of the work. The incipience, however, never becomes anything else, and we leave Colin in December in the throes of the despair of love (although he does, perhaps, project himself into the November elegy for Dido, who enjoys what Colin desires – a rebirth into a new life).

It is quite obvious, however, that the issues explored in the *Calender* exceed mere love plaints. The condition of true, requited love is, like the Golden Age, a state of bliss. The passion which

attends this love, however, leads to decay, the dissolution of
creative energy, the withering of the spirit and of nature, and
figurative death. In short, a wasted or fallen world. Colin, in
December, looks back over his growth from the innocence of
pre-lapsarian man to the wintry despair of his present state as
an unrequited lover:

> Whilome in youth, when flowrd my joyful spring,
> Like Swallow swift I wandered here and there;
> For heate of heedlesse lust me so did sting,
> That I of doubted danger had no feare:
>   I went the wastefull woodes and forest wyde,
>   Withouten dreade of Wolves to bene espyed.
>
> I wont to raunge amydde the mazie thickett,
> And gather nuttes to make me Christmas game,
> And joyed oft to chace the trembling Pricket,
> Or hunt the Hartlesse hare til she were tame.
>   What recked I of wintrye ages waste? –
>   Thos deemed I my spring would ever laste.
>
> (19-30)

He discovers, however, that his spring is not eternal and that he
along with all the other forms of nature will wither and die under
the power of mutability. The source of this grief and this decay
is of course Colin's unreturned passion for Rosalind. In *The Shepheardes Calender* this passion serves to represent the disintegration of the world which results not simply from man's submission
to the forces of nature, but more importantly from his inability
to make proper use of those forces. Cuddie, in October, recognizes that Colin ". . . were he not with love so ill bedight, / Would
mount as high, and sing as soote as Swanne". And Hobbinol, in
June, speaks of Rosalind as faithless, void of grace, "that art the
roote of all this ruthful woe!".[2]

It is not my main concern to pursue the paradox of a corrupting and redeeming love. The paradox may be resolved, however,
by the simple observation that a misused or unfulfilled passion

---

[2] See Robert Allen Durr, "Spenser's Calender of Christian Time", *ELH*,
XXIV (1958), 269-95, who argues that the primary concern of the *Calender* is the opposition between the eternal and the mutable.

represents corruption and discord, while a chaste and mutual love represents *concordia mundi*. My intention is, rather, to emphasize the latter attitude, that love is equated with redemption, and to examine the characteristics of Spenser's poetic imitation of that equation. Love in Spenser is raised poetically to a power capable of redeeming man and his fallen world, but only when it is a virtuous and mutual love – a condition which accepts the forces of life in nature but does not succumb to their infernal and disintegrating influences.

This *concordia mundi*, or perfected nature, which is the ideal aim or "cause" of so much of Spenser's poetry, "refers not merely to the human race but to the whole creation. It represents, therefore, the proper order of the universe, the systematic arrangement of all its elements according to the original intentions of God, the harmony and unity of nature and its subordination to the eternal purpose." [3] Fallen man, of whom Colin in the *Calender* is symbolic, may accomplish his restoration by obeying that natural law which maintains the proper order of the created universe. In Spenser this total order and harmony is expressed in terms of the reconciliation of opposites through love, a condition most commonly symbolized by the sacrament of marriage. Colin fails to accomplish his marriage with Rosalind and thus achieve that state of concord he is so melancholy about losing. At the end of the *Calender* he is resigned to the death which comes to him as unredeemed man. The love which Colin did not experience is, in Spenser, the power which maintains the bonds between all the levels of the Great Chain, which mediates and resolves the tension of opposites, and creates (as well as stands for) the great *concordia mundi*.

This love is, of course, as Spenser explains in Book III of *The Faerie Queene*, "Not that same which doth base affections move / In brutish mindes, and filthy lust inflame", but rather "that sweete fit that doth true beautie love, / And chooseth vertue for his dearest Dame". True beauty has an important place in Spenser's poetical expression of his world view. In "An Hymne in Honour of

---

[3] William J. Bouwsma, *Concordia Mundi: The Career and Thought of Guillaume Postel* (Cambridge, Mass., 1957), p. 64.

Beautie", it is equated with the harmonious pattern which informs the created universe:

> What time this worlds great workmaister did cast
> To make al things, such as we now behold,
> It seemes that he before his eyes had plast
> A goodly Paterne, to whose perfect mould
> He fashioned them as comely as he could;
> That now so faire and seemely they appeare,
> As nought may be amended any wheare.
>
> That wondrous Paterne wheresoere it bee,
> Whether in earth layd up in secret store,
> Or else in heaven, that no man may it see
> With sinfull eyes, for feare it to deflore,
> Is perfect Beautie which all men adore.
>
> (29-40)

For Plato, one comes to perceive pure beauty under the influence of true love. When man reaches the threshold of this ideal, he will "suddenly perceive a nature of wondrous beauty":

... a nature which in the first place is everlasting, not growing and decaying, or waxing and waning ... beauty absolute, separate, simple, and everlasting. (the *Symposium*)

This eternal and celestial Beauty is encountered in Spenser also. However, the ascent in Plato from the earthly to the celestial – which amounts to a transcendence of the earthly – is not found in Spenser's poetic vision of *concordia mundi*. In Plato, the power of love ultimately leads to the rejection of the world of nature, while in Spenser love is a force or principle which works to synthesize the discordant elements of the entire created universe (the whole range of the natural world). Love is not only a force which produces this concord, it serves also as a metaphor for the concord.

The poetic importance of Spenser's association of love with beauty and a harmonious pattern may be clarified by some of the statements of the Florentines, Pico and Ficino. Their conception of the relationship between nature and spirit is more transcendental and supernatural than Spenser's, but there is a similarity in their

ideas concerning concord. In *A Platonick Discourse Upon Love,*
Pico writes:

> Beauty . . . arises from contrariety, without which is no composition;
> it being a union of contraries, a friendly enmity, a disagreeing concord;
> whence Empedocles makes discord and concord the principles of all
> things . . . . This is Beauty in the largest sense, the same with Har-
> mony.[4]

Both Pico and Ficino express their belief that the human desire for
beauty or harmony is correctly described as love, and we would
find agreement in Spenser (love is that "sweete fit that doth true
beautie love"). In addition, the reconciliation of opposites is an
objective in both Pico and Spenser; but between nature and spirit
for the Platonist there is a division which is not characteristic of
Spenser's poetic world. The ideal of perfection or redemption in
Spenser does not normally depend on the progressive movement
upwards, renouncing what is passed, towards the apocalyptic
world. It depends, rather, on the total concord or equilibrium
between the physical and spiritual. Spenser's poetic scenes often
are refined by the influence of the divine world above, but such
a metaphorical transformation does not remove the scene from
the natural world – as these lines from "An Hymne in Honour
of Beautie" suggest:

> Thereof as every earthly thing partakes,
> Or more or lesse by influence divine,
> So it more faire accordingly it makes,
> And the grosse matter of this earthly myne,
> Which clotheth it, thereafter doth refyne.
>
> (43-47)

The distinction between Spenser's and Ficino's double conception of Venus reveals Spenser's effort to create a fictional world
in which neither the demands of nature nor the demands of spirit
are wholly absent. For Ficino there are two separate Venuses:

> . . . Venus is two-fold: one is clearly that intelligence which we said
> was in the Angelic mind; the other is the power of generation with
> which the World-Soul is endowed. Each has as consort a similar love.

---

[4]   Ed. Edmund G. Gardner (Boston, 1914), pp. 26-7.

The first, by innate love is stimulated to know the beauty of God; the second, by its love, to procreate the same beauty in bodies.[5]

These two principles, the eternal and the generative, are fused in Spenser's Venus. The "eterne in mutabilitie" of the Garden of Adonis expresses this reconciliation: the renewing, cyclically generative power of Venus is eternal in its constancy. Such a conception of fusion and harmony allows Spenser to discriminate, through his characters, scenes, and imagery, between the natural world as fallen and the natural world as redeemed. This double Venus not only stimulates sexual passion in man, but she is in command of its proper fulfillment. She creates and resolves the conflict of love. In more universal terms, this double beauty represents (as well as establishes) the harmony between the demands of nature and spirit which constitutes Spenser's perfected world or *concordia mundi*. In *The Faerie Queene*, Venus is described by Spenser as having such redemptive powers:

> Great Venus! Queene of beautie and of grace,
> The joy of Gods and men, that under skie
> Doest fayrest shine, and most adorne thy place;
> That with thy smyling looke doest pacifie
> The raging seas, and makst the stormes to flie;
> Thee, goddesse, thee the winds, the clouds doe feare,
> And, when thou spreadst thy mantle forth on hie,
> The waters play, and pleasant lands appeare,
> And heavens laugh, and all the world shews joyous cheare.[6]
>
> (4.10.44)

This ideal order does not consist of a nature rendered super-

---

[5] *Commentary on Plato's Symposium,* trans. Sears Reynolds Jayne, *University of Missouri Studies,* XIX (1944), 142.

[6] Spenser's hymn to Venus (4.10.44-47) is a translation from the hymn at the opening of Lucretius' *De rerum natura.* This classical and metaphysical conception of Venus as a principle of cosmic order seems to be appropriate for Spenser's equation of beauty (Venus), harmony, and universal concord. In addition, the Lucretian Venus is combined in the Temple of Venus passage in Book IV with the Venus who is goddess of sexual desire. This latter, courtly Venus presides over the impulse of human love; the Venus of cosmic order presides over the harmony of all forms of nature. Both conceptions of the goddess contribute to the expression of Spenser's vision of the relationship between universal concord and chaste love.

natural; it is rather the fulfillment of the potential of nature, a fulfillment wich contains the signature of the eternal world of purity. Spenser's main poetic objective is the imitation of this "embellished" world. The total vision of this *concordia mundi* is immense – perhaps as encyclopedic as Dante's; it is my intention here to isolate only that area of the poetry which deals with the issues of love (particularly the conflict of passion and purity) in order to demonstrate what part it plays in this larger vision and how it functions as extended metaphor for that *concordia mundi*.

Since the ceremony or conception of marriage is central to Spenser's use of love (although *The Faerie Queene* promises more marriages than it delivers), it will be helpful to see the range of meaning Spenser can include in a poem devoted entirely to the subject – the "Epithalamion". The domestic marriage and the terms bride and bridegroom have been often used to indicate more than a domestic unity. Origen, in his *Commentary*, interprets the Canticle of Solomon as a dramatic poem and epithalamium dealing with the union between Christ and the Church, or between Christ and the human soul (the soul as the bride and Christ as the groom).[7] All of the sacraments, according to Hugh of St. Victor, have been provided for the redemption of man; they enable him to restore the harmony between man and God destroyed by the Fall. He defines a sacrament as "a corporeal or material element set before the senses without, representing by similitude and signifying by institution and containing by sanctification some invisible and spiritual grace".[8] In his comments on marriage, Hugh applies his definition of sacrament:

If God is rightly called betrothed by Sacred Scripture and the rational spirit is spoken of as betrothed, surely there is something between God and the soul of which whatever exists in marriage between male and female is the sacrament and the image. And perhaps, to speak more specifically, the very association which is preserved externally in marriage by compact is a sacrament, and the substance of the sacra-

---

[7] See *The Song of Songs: Commentary and Homilies*, trans. R. P. Lawson, Ancient Christian Writers (London, 1957), No. 26.
[8] *On the Sacraments of the Christian Faith*, trans. Roy J. Defarrari (Cambridge, Mass., 1951), p. 155.

ment itself is the mutual love of Souls which is guarded in turn by the bond of conjugal society and agreement. And this very love again, by which male and female are united in the sanctity of marriage by their souls, is a sacrament and the sign of that love by which God is joined to the rational soul internally through the infusion of His grace and the participation of His spirit.[9]

The range of meaning Hugh develops from the marital union is two-fold. The ritual not only represents and contains the grace which links man with God, but it also represents and contains that "mutual love of souls" on the natural level. The conception of sacrament in Hugh's theology, then, is that of a metaphorical principle which extends the meaning of a central image in two directions; in this case, toward human love (eros) and divine love (agape). Such a conception is distinctly figural in that the sacrament only focuses on the human event of erotic love in order to provide the material foundation for its ultimate meaning as divine love. This figural function of the sacramental event or image is not found in Spenser. As I have suggested, the dissolution of the vertical figural line in the Renaissance in the direction of the horizontal or secular restricts the poetic representation of reality to nature and claims an almost independent sufficiency for the temporal event. There is, however, a sacramental function of imagery in Spenser's fictional world because every event or scene of that world expresses conflict or concord on a level more extensive than the immediate event or scene itself. This range of meaning extends only to the limits of the natural or created

[9]   *Ibid.*, p. 326. The familiar notion of a feminine and masculine principle in the universe is responsible, perhaps, for the ease with which the domestic union can be allegorized for metaphysical purposes. Professor Bouwsma, in his study of Postel, points out the influence of Pythagoras and Plato in promoting this cosmic sexual dualism. Postel, who was, like Spenser, acutely aware of *discordia mundi,* "conceived the basic problem of order, the problem of human nature, in terms of this dual analysis of man. *Animus* and *anima* had, through the Fall, become disarranged; they had lost their original complementary harmony; their marriage in the human soul had ended in divorce, and they could no longer engender spiritual children" (Bouwsma, p. 116). Spenser presents a striking image of concord in sex in the embrace of Amoret and Scudamour (in the rejected stanzas at the end of Book III of *The Faerie Queene*), which is likened to "that faire *Hermaphrodite*".

universe, from that dimension of nature linked to the demonic world to that level of nature linked to the divine world.

The sacrament of marriage (in the poetic rather than the religious sense), for example, in the "Epithalamion" is employed to express a total natural order or *concordia mundi* maintained by the power of love. The public sacrament of wedlock and the private sacrament of physical union are used as metaphors to represent the inclusion of man and nature in the ideal of world order. In the "Prothalamion" Spenser writes:

> Ye gentle Birdes! the worlds faire ornament,
> And heavens glorie, whom this happy hower
> Doth leade unto your lovers blisfull bower,
> Joy may you have, and gentle hearts content
> Of your loves couplement;
> And let faire Venus, that is Queene of love,
> With her heart-quelling Sonne upon you smile,
> Whose smile, they say, hath vertue to remove
> All Loves dislike, and friendships faultie guile
> For ever to assoile.
> Let endlesse Peace your stedfast hearts accord,
> And blessed Plentie wait upon your bord;
> And let your bed with pleasures chast abound,
> That fruitfull issue may to you afford.
>
> (91-104)

Venus' power to absolve love and friendship of all discord gives the poetic presentation of the marriage union a more than personal or domestic meaning. This purification motif, as well as the emphasis on the generative power of the physical union, is also found in the "Epithalamion". The combination of the regenerative and the generative – the eternal perfection of the restored world and the "fruitfull issue" which will continue that perfection – is a fundamental principle in Spenser's poetic effort to represent a reconciliation of the natural and the spiritual.

The "Epithalamion" can be divided into four sections: the masque of Hymen, during which the bride is hidden (stanzas 1-8); the appearance of the bride and the public sacrament (9-13); the bride's return home (14-16); and the preparation of the bride in the bridal bower for the final private sacrament (17-

23). A discussion of the "Epithalamion" in terms of Spenser's interest in indicating the establishment of an ordered out of a disordered world is limited by the fact that there is no fully developed contrast between order and disorder – the poem is devoted entirely to the lyric expression of harmony. In the first stanza, however, Spenser indicates the basic opposition from which the purpose of the poem develops. The mournful songs of mutability which the muses have been accustomed to sing are to be renounced in favor of the joys of love and wedlock:

> And when ye list your owne mishaps to mourne,
> Which death, or love or fortunes wreck disrayse,
> Your string could soone to sadder tenor turne,
> And teach the woods and waters to lament
> Your doleful dreriment.
> Now lay those sorrowful complaints aside;
> And having all your heads with girland crownd,
> Helpe me mine owne loves prayses to resound.
>
> (7-14)

The following seven stanzas present the masque of Hymen. The wedding day begins, in the second stanza, with the dispersion of "nights unchearefull dampe" by the "worlds light giving lampe". This removal of evil associated with darkness is thematically continued in the assertion that

> . . . lo the wished day is come at last,
> That shall, for al the paynes and sorrowes past,
> Pay to her usury of long delight.
>
> (31-33)

The bride is to be awakened and prepared for the ceremony; Hymen is anxious to begin his processional. As each detail is added throughout this section, details which increase the unity of the scene, the woods echo the variety of songs until each element of the situation blends in a musical harmony. The echo of the woods indicates the concord between physical nature and the redemptive significance of the marriage; the groom's song is echoed first, then the music of the bride's attendants as they prepare her and sing of "joy and solace". Water and wood nymphs are invoked, the main purpose of which seems to be the bringing of flowers to the scene, especially the garland of intertwined roses and lillies, symbolic of the union of sensuality and purity.

The processional continues with the introduction of the "Nymphs of Mulla" and the "lightfoot mayds" who bring to the scene the absolution of blemish and stain, and the protection of nature from malignant forces. As the bride awakens from her dreams, additional virtuous sanctions are introduced. The three Graces, handmaidens of Venus, are requested to array the bride and sing to her as they sing to Venus herself. Apollo is asked to bless this day above all others. The music of the minstrels, the pipe and tabor, "well agree withouten breach or jar". And finally:

> ... the boyes run up and downe the street,
> Crying aloud with strong confused noyce,
> As if it were one voyce,
> Hymen, ïo Hymen, Hymen they do shout;
> That even to the heavens theyr shouting shrill
> Doth reach, and all the firmament doth fill;
> To which the people standing all about,
> As in approvance, doe thereto applaud,
> And loud advaunced her laud;
> And evermore they Hymen, Hymen sing,
> That al the woods them answer, and theyr eccho ring.
>
>   (137-47)

In this procession of Hymen, this mingling of sounds and natural and supernatural figures, are a series of microcosmic representations of harmony which constitute as well as stand for the total macrocosmic concord of the central wedding. This accumulation of imagery to invoke an ideal world in which all elements agree to one purpose is the basis for Spenser's use of the ceremony of marriage as a metaphor for a redeemed natural world.

In the next section of the poem the bride makes her appearance; and before the public ritual is presented, three stanzas are devoted to a description of her external and internal beauty. Earlier in the poem the bride is associated with Venus and physical beauty; now her virginal qualities are emphasized as well. Within this bride dwells "Sweet love, and constant chastity,

/ Unspotted faith, and comely womanhood, / Regard of honour, and mild modesty". As in the Lady in *Comus*, the bride's virtue is a principle which rules "base affection", and a quality which no evil may "approach to tempt her mind to ill". The rational or divine power resides in the bride as a complement to her physical beauty. The range of association which surrounds this figure – from the most sensual to the most chaste – identifies her with both the earthly and the heavenly, and allows her to function in the "Epithalamion" as a metaphorical bond between the human and the divine. The sacraments which follow unite bride and groom in a religious and a physical act, completing Spenser's treatment of marriage harmony as an elaborate figure for a perfected nature.

The temple gates open, the bride enters to partake of the "sacred ceremonies . . . which do endless matrimony make". The ritual is attended by the roar of organs and a joyous anthem. As the holy priest performs his office, "red roses flush up" in the "pure snow" of the bride's cheeks, echoing the earlier symbolism of the lily of purity and the rose of sensual love. The sacrament ends in the familiar double harmony of the angelic music echoed by the pastoral woods. The bride is taken home in a spirit of victory, a feast is prepared and enjoyed "without restraint", indicative of the "wanton joyes" and "greedy pleasure" which will culminate in the bridal bower. Although this mood is in rather direct contrast to the religious sacrament itself, we are not to believe that these pleasures have lost divine approval, for this is a sensuality which has been purified of the imbruting power of the lower dimension of nature.

Although the woods cease their echoing response when night falls, indicating that the final union must be made silently and personally in contrast with the musical accord of the formal rite, there are still heavenly aids attending the lovers in the last section of the poem. The evening star, the "lampe of love" appears in the sky to guide them through "the nights sad dread," and an invocation is pronounced in order to purge the night of its various evils – lightning, sprights, witches, owls, ravens, ghosts, vultures. As a result of this physical union it is hoped

> That we may raise a large posterity,
> Which from the earth, which they may long possesse,
> With lasting happiness,
> Up to your haughty pallaces may mount,
> And for the guerdon of theyr glorious merit
> May heavenly tabernacles there inherit,
> Of blessed saints for to increase the count.
>
> (417-23)

The purification or regeneration of man accomplished (and represented) by the first sacrament is passed on to posterity by the generation of offspring of "glorious merit" accomplished (and represented) by the second sacrament. Thus, the final state of *concordia mundi* is produced (and symbolized) by the combination of the regenerative and generative power of love. This total harmony is suggested by Spenser at the end of the poem:

> And thou great Juno, which with awful might
> The lawes of wedlock still dost patronize,
> And the religion of the faith first plight
> With sacred rites hast taught to solemnize;
> And eeke for comfort often called art
> Of women in their smart,
> Eternally bind thou this lovely band,
> And all thy blessings unto us impart.
> And thou glad Genius, in whose gentle hand,
> The bridale bower and geniall bed remaine,
> Without blemish or staine,
> And the sweet pleasure of theyr loves delight
> With secret ayde doest succour and supply,
> Till they bring forth the fruitfull progeny,
> Send us the timely fruit of this same night.
>
> (390-404)

Spenser's metaphor of love and marriage in the "Epithalamion" serves to objectify the ideal of *concordia mundi*. This harmony consists of both the acceptance of sexual passion and the impress of the divine world. The physical beauty of the bride and the sympathetic harmony of all elemental nature constitute an approval of that sensual level of nature. And the purity of the bride and her supernatural attendants attest to the influence of a higher order within nature. The harmony of these two attitudes create an elaborate image of a perfected natural order, a natural order in which the regenerative power of love forms a lasting concord and the generative power of love prevents the return of discord through a fruitful progeny.

B. *THE FAERIE QUEENE*, BOOKS III AND IV

The content of fairy land, like the world imitated in the "Epithalamion", includes both natural and supernatural elements. There is in the world of fairy, however, a dramatic conflict as well as images of the desired reconciliation of the natural and the spiritual. Fairy land is not simply the ideal of the royal court and the battle plain on which its virtue is upheld. It includes characters, events, and scenes which are variously designed to represent the lowest as well as the highest dimension of nature. The ideal level of nature which reveals the impress of the divine is continually in conflict with the lower, corrupt level; thus, fairy land can also be said to be an imitation of the fallen world of nature which is thought to have the potential of submitting permanently to either of the two opposed levels. Since the poem is incomplete there is no single, great image of the final concord of all its conflicts (that is, no restorative reunion of all the questers at the royal court), but within the books there are incidental events and images which point clearly to the objective of a perfected natural world. Thus, it is possible to observe in Spenser's whole fictional world, or fairy land, an imitation of nature from its most demonic to its most divine aspects. In its most demonic aspect we find images of sin, death, and corruption. In its most divine aspect we find images of purity, harmony, true love, and reconciliation. It is of course this latter aspect which constitutes nature redeemed, cleansed of the impurities of sensuality, but not without the passion of love.

This redeemed world is the objective of Spenser's imitation in Books III and IV, which are treated here as a single poem. The conflict of passion and purity which governs all the elements of this poem of love is meant to be resolved in a harmony that includes something of both aspects of experience; in other words, a natural but purified love. This harmony between what reason permits and what nature demands is predicated upon the two-dimensional nature outlined in the previous chapters. The two eternal realms of the demonic and the divine which have their place below and above the cyclical world of nature are not part of Spenser's imitation here, but the impress of these two unnatural regions upon nature is made evident to the reader metaphorically. The fact that the eternal worlds of hell and heaven do not enter the poem indicates not only that the inclusive scene is the created or natural universe, but that the conflict of love must be resolved within the limits of nature by reconciling the sensual demands of passion (which is essentially a torture of the lower world), and the rational demands of chastity (which is essentially a blessing of the divine world).

The familiar Renaissance conception of an ambiguous or double nature, consisting of both that which can corrupt and that which can restore, is given poetic form in Books III and IV of *The Faerie Queene* through the ambiguity or doubleness of love. The distinction between passion and purity serves in this poetry as a metaphor for the distinction between the two levels of nature, and their reconciliation serves as a metaphor for the concord of the levels of nature. This distinction between the wholly sensual and the wholly chaste corresponds to the doubleness of love, for love may be associated either with the corruptions of sensuality or the purity of chastity.

In addition, the Renaissance conception of man as *compositum mixtum* provides some degree of evidence for contending that a two-dimensional concept of love may serve as a metaphor for a two-dimensional nature, and that the harmonizing of this doubleness in love may serve as a metaphor for the desired harmonious order of nature. The *compositum mixtum* doctrine presents an image of man which has two faces in precisely the same way as nature has two faces, divided between a level of discord and chaos and a level of elemental concord and order. The natural world in which man actually lives reveals a conflict between two levels, with the desired objective the fulfillment of the potential of concord and order within nature. Similarly, man, according to the doctrine of *compositum mixtum*, exists in a mediate position between the brutish and the angelic, the sensual and the rational, the passionate and the totally chaste, partaking of the qualities of both extremes of the oppositions. This split in man not only accounts for the conflicts of life, but it provides the basis for the reconciliation of the discordant capacities. The angelic capacity qualifies and redeems the brutish; the rational qualifies and redeems the sensual; and most important for the argument here, the virtue of chastity qualifies and redeems sexual passion, resulting in a chaste, pure, or true love. This chaste love consists of a virtuous reconciliation of the double demands within man, and therefore of the two levels of nature because wanton sexual passion identifies the lower dimension of nature and absolute chastity or purity the upper dimension.

It is significant that the lowest region of fairy land in these two books is represented by the House of Busirane, and the highest by the Temple of Venus. The sufferings brought about by Cupid in the House of Busirane take place in the hellish, tortuous region at the boundary between the lowest level of nature and the demonic world below. The realm of the queen of "beautie and of grace" is located at the boundary between the highest level of nature and the divine world above. Love may either corrupt or purify. Spenser's objective is to purify the world through love, a chaste love which brings the natural world into alignment with the spiritual, but does not renounce a "natural felicity".

Spenser's theme of the removal of discord through love, and the poetic heightening of this theme to include the concord or redemption of all nature is expressed in a romantic fictional mode. The ordinary laws of nature are often suspended in order to allow the characters to perform acts uncommon to man. The heroes and heroines are superior in degree to common man, but they are not gods; they remain heightened types of human kind. As such, the world of fairy reflects a displacement from the totally mythic world, but not so much that ordinary empirical reality is the foundation of its experiences, or that the poetic marvelous cannot be admitted to the action and the imagery. The romantic mode, to refer back to Frye, reveals "the tendency to suggest implicit mythical patterns in a world more closely associated with human experience". The displacement of the mythic world can be viewed in Spenser also as a displacement of the supernatural in the direction of the cyclical world of nature, or a displacement of the figural representation of reality in the direction of a more secular representation of reality. To replace the apotheosis of man or the absorption of nature by heaven, we find the fulfillment of man and nature fully within the temporal, mutable world.

The *aventures* of Spenser's poem of love, which convey the conflict between the demonic aspect of nature (wanton sexuality) and the divine aspect of nature (chastity), center around three love quests: Britomart's for Artegall, Scudamour's for Amoret, and Florimell's for Marinell. The theme of the two books is not the fulfillment of the double virtue of chastity-friendship, but rather the conflict between passion and purity and the resolution of that conflict by an equilibrium of opposites which is in accord with both nature and spirit. Chastity in Spenser, with the exception of Belphoebe, is not a renunciation of the flesh or nature, but a condition by which proper use of the flesh or nature is made. The ultimate supremacy of this chastity in fairy land, in other words, constitutes that desired perfection of nature or the harmony between the drives of life and the requirements of the divine law. Both chastity, or what should be called chaste love, and friendship, which is the "mutual love of souls", constitute Spenser's ideal of true love; it is a force capable of transforming the discord of the contradictory aspects of experience into a concord. This ideal of true love, however, functions in the poem as something larger than a personal and domestic harmony; it becomes an extensive metaphor for the ideal of universal concord established out of seemingly unreconcilable levels of existence. This principle of a discordant concord harmonizes the sufferings of sensual passion with the divine purity of the virginal in the love adventures of the poem. It harmonizes, also, in the Garden of Adonis, the generative and the eternal (and in the Mutabilitie Cantos change becomes a function of eternal order). Just as the image of marriage in the "Epithalamion" is used sacramentally to extend the range of meaning from personal concord to *concordia mundi*, the image of chaste love and the conflicts leading to its affirmation are used metaphorically to express concord and discord on a level more universal than the immediate scenes and events themselves.

The three central love quests provide a certain amount of orderly narrative in the poem, for there is a pattern of action which first prevents and then allows a reconciliation of the heroines and their lovers. However, Spenser's more obvious form of organization is the creation of an intricate design of conflict and reconciliation, rather than the development of a progressive dramatic action of beginning, middle, and end. This design is made up of a variety of incident and image in which either the conflict between the sensual and the virginal or their harmonious reconciliation is expressed. The fact that Spenser very often ignores a chronological sequence of actions, or that he seems little interested in any kind of sequence of events, suggests that the key to the structure of this poem is not to be found in the progression of its events and images, but rather in their design. The kind of love, for example, described in the Temple of Venus (Book IV) provides an effective ending for the poem, but the union of Amoret and Scudamour which takes place there actually occurs before Amoret's captivity in the House of Busirane (Book III). This neglect of the dramatic sequence of events in Books III and IV may be due to the fragmentary nature of the whole *Faerie Queene*, according to the plan of which the action would indeed proceed from a beginning at the royal court, through a middle of redemptive quests, and finally to complete reconciliation back at the court. Spenser's obvious method in this poem of creating a design of conflict and reconciliation rather than a progressive action enables one, however, to isolate these books from the others, and to reject the implication in the letter to Ralegh that no part of the poem is complete until the final reunion with Gloriana. Such a reunion would have only reinforced what is quite effective in Books III and IV already. My analysis of this poem of love, therefore, will emphasize the tapestry-like design rather than a dramatic unity, with the intention of clarifying Spenser's theme of the redemption of nature as it is expressed through the extended metaphor of chaste love or the harmony of the sensual and the virginal.

The three quests are searches for chaste love, but surrounding this action are a variety of incidents and images which define, reinforce, and counter the main objective of the entire imitation. First, the Timias and Belphoebe episode (3.5.27-55). The curative motif which appears throughout the poem is presented in this episode as Belphoebe restores Timias to health after being wounded in battle. Belphoebe, who is described as having mysterious restorative powers, takes the healed Timias to her "earthly Paradize" where he suffers a second wound – the wound of love. He is tortured primarily by the shame of loving someone so virginal; but his pain is relieved finally by the recognition of the equation between Belphoebe and the virgin rose, the flower which bears the "fruit of honour and all chast desyre". Belphoebe stands on the "highest stayre / Of th' honorable stage of womanhead", and thus functions in the poem as the human counterpart of that divine purity which must temper sexual passion in order to produce chaste love.

Second, the description of the goddess of discord, Até (4.1.19-30). Até has her origin in the infernal regions of the world. She is associated with darkness, barrenness, thorns, decay, the defilement of the holy, and the strife of nations, men, and lovers. Her great task is to break that "great golden chaine" which "Concord hath together tide". The description is important as a demonic counterpart to Spenser's poetic objective of *concordia mundi*.

Third, the Canacee and Triamond story (4.2.30-54; 4.3.1-52). The unity of the three souls of the three brothers in the single brother Triamond is a metaphysical allegory of friendship or the "mutual love of souls", an important part of Spenser's pattern of concord of lovers, all men, and nature. The battle strife between Cambell and Triamond is resolved by Cambine who enters complete with magic wand, uroboric snake, and a cup of Nepenthe, a drink of "soverayne grace" which redeems man and prepares him for apotheosis. The strife ends, typically, in the double marriage of Triamond and Canacee, and Cambell and Cambine.

And finally, the tournament for Florimell's girdle (4.4.1-48, 4.5.1-26). The girdle is an important symbol of that true love to which the poem is devoted. It is referred to as the girdle of Venus or the girdle of chaste love; it was originally given to Florimell "to bind lascivious desire, / And loose affections streightly to restraine". The third day of the tournament is won by Britomart who restores the girdle to the knights of Mayden-head. Supporting the correlation between chaste love and a re-deemed nature, this return of the girdle is likened to the coming of water to the waste land.

The quest of Britomart for Artegall is important on two levels: the personal and the political, or what might be called the ro-mantic and the heroical. There are to be two results from the marriage of Britomart and Artegall. The union will not only fulfill Britomart's personal quest for true love in order to cure her wound of passion, but it will also generate a line of heroes whose accomplishments will be a series of political redemptions culmi-nating in the British Tudor dynasty. This merger of a personal destiny on the level of love and a national destiny on the level of politics is evident in many places in Spenser's poem; it is a harmony of romantic and heroic goals which reinforce each other and extend the meaning of the poem to a universal level. Chastity is an active and a warfaring virtue leading to a personal fulfill-ment in chaste love; as such, it is paralleled by the warfare which leads to the establishment of the ideal state. In addition, the ideal of chaste love is not only associated with political purification through Britomart and Artegall, but also with the concord of all nature as expressed in the Garden of Adonis and the Temple of Venus. Thus, Spenser suggests a total union on the personal, political, and natural levels.

Britomart's story begins with her vision of Artegall seen in the mirror of Venus (made by Merlin). He appears to her

> . . . revealed in a mirrhour playne;
> Whereof did grow her first engraffed payne,
> Whose root and stalke so bitter yet did taste,

> That but the fruit more sweetness did contayne,
> Her wretched dayes in dolour she mote waste,
> And yield the pray of love to lothsome death at last.
>
> (3.2.17)

In these lines Spenser indicates a major pattern of imagery in the poem. Love is associated with both death and sweetness. The pain of passion is deathlike; but Venus, "Soone as with fury thou doest them inspire, / In generation seeke to quench their inward fire" (4.10.46). Throughout the poem these two worlds of death and sweetness are separated from each other and come to be associated, respectively, with the demonic and divine aspects of nature. The mirror itself suggests a similar view of the world. It is "like to the world itselfe," and is capable of showing "Whatever thing was in the world contayned, / Betwixt the lowest earth and the hevens hight" (3.2.19). This glass world, like the poem itself, reflects the created universe.

Britomart's passion for Artegall is distinguished, in spite of the pain it causes her, from a baser desire:

> Not that she lusted after any one,
> For she was pure from blame of sinfull blott;
> Yet wist her life at last must lincke in that same knot.
>
> (3.2.23)

Or as her attendant, Glaucé, remarks after observing the effect the vision of Artegall has on Britomart:

> Of much more uncouth thing I was affrayd,
> Of filthy lust, contrary unto kind;
> But this affection nothing straunge I finde;
> For who with reason can you aye reprove
> To love the semblaunt pleasing most your minde,
> And yield your heart whence ye cannot remove?
> No guilt in you, but in the tyranny of love.
>
> (3.2.40)

Although Britomart's passion is not lustful, it nevertheless holds her in a tortuous bondage; and her sufferings are similar to those of Amoret and Florimell who are held in bondage by figures who represent a lustful passion. Introduced here is one of the most important issues of the poem: how to break the tyranny of passion without submitting to the corruptions of wanton sensuality. The fulfillment of Britomart's personal destiny requires her to submit to love but not to renounce her purity. Such an objective is accomplished in a chaste union with Artegall.

The wound of love festers in Britomart; it "rankleth in this same fraile fleshly mould, / That all my entrailes flow with poisnous gore, / And th' ulcer groweth daily more and more" (3.2. 39). A curative is needed; Britomart must be redeemed of the corruption and figurative death caused by her desire for Artegall. The herbs employed by Glaucé to abate the desire and produce barrenness are of no avail, and Britomart becomes "like a pyned ghost . . . which long hath waited by the Stygian strond" (3.2.52). The only cure is union with Artegall. Love can redeem the suffering that love has caused. This irony is necessary in Spenser's poem, for not only is there a double dimension to nature, corruption and disorder opposed to purity and concord, but there is a double dimension to love. The dimension which has the approval of the poet in both cases is, of course, that rational and virtuous order which has its origin in the *lex aeterna*.

> For were no law in love, but all that lust
> Might them oppresse, and painefully turmoile,
> His kingdome would continue but a while.
>
> (6.8.23)

The law of Cupid which prevents the pain and corruption of lust is parodied in the House of Busirane where another kind of Cupid maintains his power:

> Lo! now the hevens obey to me alone,
> And take me for their Jove, whiles Jove to earth is gone.
>
> (3.11.35)

Evil is this Cupid's good, and the ironic ambiguity between this love and the love which establishes concord is exploited in Spenser's poem to show that the forces of nature may either corrupt or redeem, depending on whether they are aligned with the demonic or the divine.

Britomart and Glaucé, seeking some relief for Britomart's wound of love, visit the Cave of Merlin. Here Britomart is told by Merlin that a union with Artegall is necessary, and that a universal peace will result from their marriage by cause of their "famous progeny", a line of heroes whose mission it will be to bring civil harmony to the world. Merlin's function is not only to convince Britomart that it is a "hevenly destiny" for her to seek and marry Artegall, but also to inform her that her own personal restoration in love will be reinforced over the centuries by the great restoration of decayed kingdoms and usurped crowns, culminating in the reign of the Tudor virgin queen. To direct nature and her agents toward such a universal order is a familiar function for the magician in the Renaissance. According to Cassirer, in his study of Pico, the true magician understands that divine law which binds heaven to earth and can direct nature toward that objective of concord.[10] Merlin, like Bacon's poet, is capable of joining that which nature hath severed and severing that which nature hath joined:

> For he by wordes could call out of the sky
> Both Sunne and Moone, and make them him obey;
> The Land to sea, and sea to maineland dry,
> And darksom night he eke could turne to day.
>
> (3.3.12)

He appears to be that kind of magician who understands the divine law which maintains nature in an alignment with spirit, for he prophesies for Britomart a chaste love and a future civil restoration of nobility and virtue.

Merlin observes that the outcome of Britomart's quest for Artegall will be restorative, but it will begin in pain and fear:

> For so must all things excellent begin;
> And eke enrooted deepe must be that Tree,
> Whose big embodied braunches shall not lin
> Till they to hevens hight forth stretched bee:
> For from thy wombe a famous Progenee
> Shall spring out of the auncient Trojan blood,

---

[10] See "Giovanni Pico della Mirandola", *Journal of the History of Ideas*, III (1942), 338-39. Note also C. S. Lewis' distinction between the optimistic assumption in magic of human omnipotence, and the pessimistic assumption in astrology of human impotence: *English Literature in the Sixteenth Century* (London, 1954), pp. 5-13.

Which shall revive the sleeping memoree
Of those same antique Peres, the hevens brood,
Which Greeke and Asian rivers stayned with their blood.

Renowmed kings, and sacred Emperours,
Thy fruitful Ofspring, shall from thee descend;
Brave Captaines, and most mighty warriors,
That shall their conquests through all lands extend,
And their decayed kingdomes shall amend:
The feeble Britons, broken with long warre,
They shall upreare, and mightily defend
Against their forren foe that commes from farre,
Till universall peace compound all civill jarre.

(3.3.22-3)

This promise of political concord is reinforced by Merlin with a long account of the civil restorations which will be effected by Artegall and his noble progeny. The range of allusion and the scope of this prophecy of an ideal state suggest that the universal civil peace is a vision of the total perfection of human history on the political level. The content of this vision, however, is bound up with Britomart's personal, romantic quest to heal her wound of love in a chaste union with Artegall. Thus, the resolution of civil strife and love strife are linked. The objective is both a perfection of nature on the historical or political level, and a perfection of nature in terms of the conflict between passion and purity. Both redemptions contribute to the establishment of the ideal of *concordia mundi*. In addition, the two principles of regeneration and generation are involved here, as in the "Epithalamion". The regeneration of the "decayed kingdomes" and the regeneration or rebirth of Britomart into the world of chaste love are both supplemented by the generation of noble offspring who will prevent the return of corruption and pain in either politics or love.

Britomart's first experience on her quest for chaste love is at the Castle Joyous. The corrupt sensuality of this place and the wanton nature of the Lady of Delight, Malecasta, give Britomart her first taste of the world of love she has decided to enter. Her initiation into love begins with an education in the evils of sensual delight. There is no doubt, of course, about the outcome of

Britomart's visit to this castle of joy, for her enchanted spear and the divine virtue of chastity which reside within her serve as permanent protection against the demonic aspects of the natural world. But it is necessary to the design of the poem that the complexity of passion be made evident. Sensuality is not meant to be rejected in the pursuit of love, but the wantonness of this castle is, for it shows no mark of the stamp of the divine world.

In addition to presenting Britomart to the world of sensuality, the Castle Joyous also introduces the story of Venus and Adonis, which is such an important part of Spenser's design in his poem of love. The story is portrayed on a tapestry of the castle, beginning with the first moments of Venus' passion for Adonis, and ending with his death and transformation into a flower. Although the story is used here to express the bitter and painful nature of sexual passion, emphasizing Cupid's wound in conjunction with the wound of the boar, the continuation of this tale in Canto VI in which Adonis is said not to be dead but continually enjoyed by Venus, suggests that Spenser had a further use for this myth. The wounded but restored god provides Spenser with a narrative of regeneration on the mythic level which reinforces his theme of regeneration on a more natural level. The knights of fairy land who are wounded by battle and by love are the counterparts in the romantic mode of the wounded Adonis in the mythic mode. Fairy land is a fictional world displaced from the mythic, but the world of myth is employed there, significantly muted by tapestries and poetic metaphor. Adonis is, as Miss Weston points out, a "principle of animate Nature, upon whose preservation, and unimpaired energies, the life of man, directly, and indirectly, depends".[11] The impairment or wound of Adonis corresponds to the wasting of the world of nature, or to the "decayed king-domes". This aspect of the myth is made clear in the Garden of Adonis where the continual regeneration of the god provides eternal fruitfulness for the world of nature. In addition to the

[11] *From Ritual to Romance* (New York, Anchor Books, 1957), pp. 43-4. See also A. C. Hamilton, "Spenser's Treatment of Myth", *ELH,* XXVI (1959), 346-52.

restoration of fallen kingdoms and the whole range of nature, Adonis as the eternally renewed object of Venus' love supplies a principle of regeneration in love.

That part of Britomart's initiation into the regenerative and generative life of love which involves the rejection of wanton sensuality is succesfully accomplished. Her next task is described at the end of Book III when she undertakes the rescue of Amoret from the House of Busirane. This scene is the world of experience in love; the images with which it is described identify it as the natural world's counterpart to the eternal world of the demonic. Its dungeons are located on that boundary between the lowest dimension of nature and hell. Amoret is

> ... cruelly pend
> In dolefull darknes from the view of day,
> Whilest deadly torments doe her chast brest rend,
> And the sharp steele doth rive her hart in tway.
>
> (3.11.11)

Scudamour desires the release of Amoret from this captivity, but feels helpless in the face of such power as Busirane has:

> What boots it plaine that cannot be redrest,
> And sow vaine sorrow in a fruitlesse eare,
> Sith powre of hand, nor skill of learned brest,
> Ne worldly price, cannot redeeme my deare
> Out of her thraldome and continuall feare:
> For he, the tyrant, which her hath in ward
> By strong enchauntments and blacke Magicke leare,
> Hath in a dungeon deepe her close embard,
> And many dreadfull feends hath pointed to her gard.
>
> There he tormenteth her most terribly
> And day and night afflicts with mortall paine,
> Because to yield to him love she doth deny.
>
> (3.11.16-17)

Busirane is a type of evil seducer, and is associated with the familiar Renaissance libertine arguments for perverse love. The libertine is a demonic figure in the intellectual and poetic tradition relevant here; his realm is the lower dimension of nature, and what he represents is expressed in terms of corruption, sin,

and death. Amoret's bondage in this world portrays the enthrall-
ment of man by wanton sensuality which pulls him down toward
the demonic and away from the divine or the possibility of a
chaste love. Her release from this region and her reunion with
Scudamour is accomplished by Britomart. This act redeems
Amoret from the sensual dimension of nature and allows her to
establish a chaste love with Scudamour. The emergence of this
chaste love, however, is more than a solution to a personal problem of love; the destruction of the level of nature represented by
the House of Busirane separates the passion of love from corruption and allows it to combine with the virtue of chastity, a
process which symbolizes the redemption of nature or the realignment of the natural world with the divine law.

The adventures at the House of Busirane are important for
both Amoret and Britomart. Amoret, who already has been united
with Scudamour in the Temple of Venus (although this does not
appear in the poem until Book IV), is in a state of figurative
death, expressed through the demonic imagery of the dungeon
and torture. She does not have the power to accomplish her own
resurrection from this condition and the subsequent rebirth into
the world of chaste love. Her salvation is accomplished by
Britomart, and by performing this act Britomart herself has
succeeded in another task placed before her in her quest for the
chaste love of Artegall – "for lovers heaven must passe by sor-
rowes hell". The power of Britomart's chastity is proved by her
ability to part the flames guarding the entrance to the House of
Busirane, an analogy to Christ's harrowing of hell. After passing
through the fire and entering the arcanum, Britomart discovers
the meaning of this region from the tapestries and the masque
of Cupid.

On the tapestries Cupid is presented as a demonic figure, in
competition with the great Jove:

> . . . all Cupids warres they did repeate,
> And cruell battailes, which he whilome fought
> Gainst all the Gods to make his empire great;
> Besides the huge massacres, which he wrought
> On mighty kings and kesars into thraldome brought.

Therein was writt how often thondring Jove
Had felt the point of his hart-percing dart.

(3.11.29-30)

The corrupting power of sensual love extends from the personal
pain of lovers to the destruction of kingdoms, and to the discord
of all nature. Spenser gathers together the elements of the whole
microcosm – man, the state, and physical nature – into a single
world which reveals the corruptions of love, but which has the
potential of being redeemed by love. The ravages of love pictured
in the tapestries are summarized:

Kings, Queenes, Lords, Ladies, knights, and Damsels gent,
Were heap'd together with the vulgar sort,
And mingled with the raskall rablement,
Without respect of person or of port,
To shew Dan Cupids powre and great effort:
And round about a border was entrayled
Of broken bowes and arrowes shivered short;
And a long bloody river through them rayld,
So lively and so like that living sence it fayld.

(3.11.46)

In a further chamber Britomart discovers the idol of Cupid and
the motto "Bee bold". She remains in the furthest room until
nightfall, when

With that an hideous storme of winde arose,
With dreadfull thunder and lightning atwixt,
And an earthquake, as if it streight would lose
The world's foundations from his centre fixt.

(3.12.2)

The masque of Cupid which follows, portraying the painful nature
of love, is thus associated with the elemental disruption of all
nature. The demonic aspect of love, identified with the lowest
dimension of nature, causes discord throughout the entire natural
world. The masque itself is a procession of figures representing
those qualities associated with the unregenerate side of love: desire, fear, hope, grief, pleasure and displeasure, cruelty; Cupid
himself followed by reproach, repentance, shame; and finally
aspects of discord such as strife, inconstant change, dread of
heaven, ending at last with "Death with infamy".

Britomart enters the room from which the procession issued and discovers Busirane attempting to seduce Amoret. She drives him off, is wounded by him in the fight, and persuaded by Amoret not to kill him because only he can release her from her bondage. While the knights in this poem of love are romantic counterparts to the mythic Adonis, Busirane is the romantic counterpart to the mythic Cupid. His wounding of Britomart represents the injury of sensuality she must suffer in her initiation into chaste love (previously indicated by the pain caused by the image of Artegall in the mirror). This ambiguous nature of love, or the ambiguous function of Cupid-Busirane, is reinforced by the fact that the release from the pain of love (Amoret's captivity) can only be accomplished by Busirane. Britomart forces him to reverse his charms, symbolizing the revocation of wanton sensuality necessary for redemption in true love; Amoret is released, and her wound closes up. The reversal of Busirane's influence also dissolves the idol, the motto, the masque, and the tapestries of Cupid.

The reunion which takes place between Amoret and Scudamour at this point is described in those five stanzas rejected by Spenser as a conclusion to Book III. It appears as if a reunion here was sacrificed in favor of the original union of the two lovers which has taken place earlier in time, but which is described later at the end of Book IV. The rejected stanzas are important, however, as an expresson of concord, vividly conveyed by that image of the hermaphrodite already noted:

> So seemd those two, as growne together quite,
> That Britomart halfe envying their blesse,
> Was much empassioned in her gently sprite,
> And to her selfe oft wisht like happiness,
> In vaine she wisht, that fate n'ould let her yet possesse.[12]

[12] The foetal incest of the twins Argante and Ollyphant parodies this image of concord: "Ere they into the lightsom world were brought, / In fleshly lust were mingled both yfere, / And in that monstrous wise did to the world appere." (3.7.48)

This is a concord seen from the perspective of the demonic. The fact that it has an ironic similarity to the hermaphroditic concord indicates Spenser's interest in distinguishing corrupt from purified sensuality.

Not only is a concord of the male and female principles expressed in the rejected stanzas, but also Britomart's desire for such a union in her personal life. The image of the hermaphrodite does convey the personal love union of Amoret and Scudamour, but it also has a range of meaning beyond the personal, in the direction of the total concord of nature through the harmony of the principles of anima and animus. The figure of Hermaphrodite provides an image for the union of lovers in chaste love, which in turn serves as an image for concord on a more extensive level. The image is, in addition, another example of Spenser's technique of reinforcing and enlarging the meaning of a personal love experience by introducing a figure from the mythic world.

Britomart's final appearance in this poem of love occurs in the middle of Book IV when she and Artegall meet, first in battle, then in love. The warfare between Britomart and Artegall serves as a metaphor for the contention which makes love a form of strife:

> Ah, cruell hand! and thrise more cruell hart,
> That workst such wrecke on her to whom thou dearest art!
>
> What yron courage ever could endure
> To work such outrage on so faire a creature;
> And in his madnesse think with hands impure
> To spoyle so goodly workmanship of nature,
> The maker selfe resembling in her feature!
> Certes some hellish furie or some feend
> This mischiefe framd for their first loves defeature,
> To bath their hands in bloud of dearest freend,
> Thereby to make their loves beginning their lives end.
> (4.6.16-17)

A contentious love, however, is demonic, and characteristically associated with the fiend and fury of hell. In metaphoric opposition to this strife is the beauty of Britomart, representing the perfection of nature and carrying the stamp of the divine. When her helmet is removed, she becomes "That peerelesse paterne of Dame Nature's pride / And heavenly image of perfection". She is worshipped as "some celestiall vision" (4.6.24). The equation of Britomart and a perfect pattern of nature recalls Spenser's similar description of Venus in "An Hymne in Honour of Beautie". In that poem and in the Temple of Venus passage of Book IV, Venus is also described in terms comparable to the goddess Nature in the *Mutabilitie Cantos*. Britomart may be thought of as the natural, romantic counterpart of the Venus / Nature divinity by virtue of the harmony of the forces of nature and the divine within her, expressed by her capacity for chaste love.[13]

When Britomart discovers that her foe has been Artegall, "Her hart did leape, and all her hart-strings tremble, / For sudden joy and secret feare withall". The combination of joy and fear is an important part of Spenser's pattern of Britomart's initiation into love. She desires the transformation from maid to woman, and the fufillment of Merlin's prophecy of regeneration; but this desire is accompanied by a fear of sensuality, a fear which has diminished in the course of her adventures at the Castle Joyous and the House of Busirane. Love, however, cannot be avoided by either Britomart or Artegall. As Glaucé remarks to him:

> And you, Sir Artegall, the salvage knight,
> Henceforth may not disdaine that womans hand
> Hath conquered you anew in second fight:
> For whylome they have conquerd sea and land,
> And heaven it selfe, that nought may them withstand.
> Ne henceforth be rebellious unto love,
> That is the crowne of knighthood, and the band
> Of noble minds derived from above,
> Which being knit with vertue, never will remove.
>
> (4.6.31)

The union of the two lovers which takes place at this point is a fulfillment of that bond "derived from above", or chaste love. They part immediately, however, and the reader is left to be satisfied with this less than formal marriage (which never occurs in *The Faerie Queene* as it stands).

Britomart's love quest is nevertheless completed. And it is a regenerative process on many levels. It has healed the wound of passion in Britomart herself, and constitutes her rebirth into a

[13] See J. W. Bennett, "Spenser's Venus and the Goddess Nature of the *Cantos of Mutabilitie*", *Studies in Philology*, XXX (1933), pp. 160-92.

condition of chaste love. In addition, it promises the generation of redeemed offspring who will bring about the restoration of the state. And in the chastening but not the renunciation of sexual desire, the world of nature in general is purified of its disruptive elements. The power of chaste love, then, restores the world to a state of perfection, for the demonic aspects of nature are removed and the resulting condition aligns the natural world with the requirements of the divine law.

A similar love tension between Florimell and Marinell is resolved, in the undersea regions of Tryphon, more by accident than by any concerted effort, although Florimell is in search of Marinell. Marinell has rejected love as a result of Proteus' prophecy to his mother, Cymoent. Proteus has warned

> . . . from womankind to keepe him well,
> For of a woman he should have much ill;
> A virgin straunge and stout should dismay or kill.
>
> (3.4.25)

He is therefore brought up by his mother to be an enemy of love, and to glorify himself in fairy land as a fearless knight in battle. The prophecy is fulfilled in part by Britomart's wounding of Marinell, the beginning of his initiation into the ambiguous pain and bliss of love. Nothing seems able to cure Marinell of this wound, and he is carried back to the kingdom of Tryphon by his mother, who has found him injured in fairy land.

> . . . up him taking in their tender hands,
> They easely unto her charett beare:
> Her teme at her commaundement quiet stands,
> Whiles they the corse into her wagon reare,
> And strowe with flowres the lamentable beare.
> Then all the rest into their coches clim,
> And through the brackish waves their passage sheare;
> Upon great Neptunes necke they softly swim,
> And to her watry chamber swiftly carry him.
>
> (3.4.42)

Marinell is an Adonis-knight, whose figurative death provokes the elegiac tone of this stanza and prepares us for his later rebirth into the world of true love.

Florimell, in the meantime, is pursued by the lustful, representing the beginning of her initiation into love. Her brief experience with the witch and her son serves as a demonic parallel
to the relationship between Marinell and Cymoent. Both Marinell
and the witch's son experience a love wound caused by Florimell.
In addition, both Cymoent and the witch attempt to cure the
love wound by securing Florimell for their suffering offspring.
The witch employs a hyena-like beast who feeds "on womens
flesh" to chase and capture Florimell for her son. Cymoent asks
Proteus to release Florimell from bondage in order to relieve
Marinell's pain. There is a contrast, of course, between the beast
and the lust of the witch's son, and the more chaste passion
which Florimell and Marinell have for each other. The ironic
comparison between the two situations points up the universality
of the pain of love and the necessity for its cure. It also distinguishes between false and true love, or the corrupt and pure
aspects of the same desire. The ambiguity is reinforced by the
witch's creation, in a "secret mew", of a false Florimell to "heale
her sonne whose senses were decayd" (4.8.4). This demonic
counterpart to the true Florimell has for a soul, significantly,
one of the spirits who fell with the "Prince of Darkeness".

Florimell escapes the beast by taking refuge with a fisherman,
who also attempts to seduce her. She is rescued by Proteus, taken
to his undersea cave, and emprisoned in a dungeon for refusing
to submit to his advances.

> For wall'd it was with waves, which rag'd and ror'd
> As they the cliffe in peeces would have cleft;
> Besides ten thousand monsters foule abhor'd
> Did waite about it, gaping griesly, all begor'd.
>
> And in the midst thereof did horror dwell,
> And darkenesse dredd that never viewed day,
> Like to the balefull house of lowest hell.
>
>   (4.11.3-4)

The lower world is invoked again by Spenser to characterize the
perversion of true love. Marinell, in the meantime, has been cured
of Britomart's wound, and now joins Cymoent in the Hall of
Proteus to witness the great watery procession celebrating the

marriage of the Thames and the Medway. This concord of rivers contributes to Spenser's theme of regeneration throughout the natural world because of the fruitful generation associated with the waters. The procession provides an opportunity to

> ... recount the Seas posterity:
> So fertile be the flouds in generation,
> So huge their numbers, and so numberlesse their nation.
>
> Therefore the antique wisards well invented
> That Venus of the fomy sea was bred,
> For that the seas by her are most augmented.
>   (4.12.1-2)

The fertility of the waters in the concord of the Thames and the Medway reinforces and extends the meaning of the regenerative power of love (through the allusion to Venus), the fertility of all the marriages in the poem, and the effects of that fertility on the destiny of Britain.

After the marriage procession in the Hall of Proteus, Florimell laments her condition:

> For heaven, that unto all lends equall eare,
> Is farre from hearing of my heavy plight;
> And lowest hell, to which I lie most neare,
> Cares not what evils hap to wretched wight.
>   (4.12.6)

She has described her location as at the limit of the natural world, closest to the eternal world of corruption and death that is hell, and furthest from the upper reaches of nature which lie upon the boundary of the divine world. These levels of nature are, of course, identified by the damnation and the salvation of love, or corruption in sensuality and redemption in chaste desire. Florimell's release from this lower region comes after Cymoent's appeal to Proteus to free her in order that her son's wound of love may be cured – a second wound suffered when he overhears Florimell's love lament. Both Florimell and Marinell are between life and death because of love; she because of her bondage by the lustful Proteus, and he because of his unfulfilled passion for Florimell. Their mutual rebirth occurs in their mutual union.

Proteus frees Florimell for Marinell, and Marinell

> Who soone as he beheld that angels face
> Adorn'd with all divine perfection,
> His cheared heart eftsoones away gan chace
> Sad death, revived with her sweet inspection,
> And feeble spirit inly felt refection:
> As withered weed through cruell winters time,
> That feeles the warmth of sunny beames reflection,
> Lifts up his head that did before decline,
> And gins to spread his leafe before the faire sunshine.
>
> (4.12.34)

The former equation of love and death is now transformed to an equation of love and restoration, characterized by the rejuvenation of the vegetable world in the time of spring. The release of Florimell, the rebirth of Marinell, the coming of fertility to the land unite in an image of redemption through chaste love – part of the design of Spenser's tapestry of *concordia mundi*.

The story of Scudamour and Amoret, the third main love quest in this poem of love, involves not only the two lovers but also Belphoebe and the two regions which govern the meaning of the whole work: the Garden of Adonis and the Temple of Venus. The twins, Amoret and Belphoebe, were immaculately conceived and born in the time of spring of Chrysogonee (the daughter of Amphisa, or "having a double nature"). Between them they share "the heritage of all celestial grace". Venus, in search of Cupid, comes upon "the secret haunts of Dianes company". A repetition of the historic contention between these two goddesses seems to be assured, but Venus firmly states: "We both are bownd to follow heavens behests, / And tend our charges with obeisaunce meek" (3.6.22). Together they seek the lost Cupid and discover, instead, the infant twins Amoret and Belphoebe.

> Dame Phoebe to a Nymphe her babe betooke
> To be brought up in perfect Maydenhed,
> And, of her selfe, her name Belphoebe red:
> But Venus hers thence far away convayd,
> To be upbrought in goodly womanhed;
> And, in her little loves stead, which was strayd,
> Her Amoretta cald, to comfort her dismayd.
>
> (3.6.28)

Amoret is raised in Venus' paradise, the Garden of Adonis. This region is Spenser's imitation of a perfected nature, an image of concord toward which all discord in the poem points. The two dimensions of nature are fused in this garden, that which is cyclical and mutable and that which is eternal and ordered according to the divine plan. The theme of the redemption of nature in Renaissance poetry is based upon the effort of the age to formulate a particular kind of continuity between the world of nature and the world of spirit. This continuity is best described as an alignment of the two worlds in which nature is suffused with the values of the divine world but still maintains the identity of its own natural demands. The Garden of Adonis expresses, perhaps more effectively than any other single passage in Renaissance poetry, that alignment of the mutable world with the eternal principle of the divine world. It serves as a paradigm for the reconciliation of the discordant forces in this poem of love.

The Old Genius who guards the double gates of the garden which release man and matter to the world and readmit them when they are spent, has himself a double function. He first clothes "a thousand naked babes" with "fleshly weeds", signifying the fall of man from the earthly paradise, then

> After that they againe retourned beene,
> They in that Gardin planted bee agayne,
> And grow afresh, as they had never seene
> Fleshly corruption, nor mortal payne.
>
> (3.6.33)

The garden is a region of "eternal return", a place where the matter of nature originates and to which it returns for renewal. The distinction is made, however, between substance and form, between that which is eternal and that which is born and dies:

> That substaunce is eterne, and bideth so;
> Ne when the life decayes and forme does fade,
> Doth it consume and into nothing goe,
> But chaunged is, and often altred to and froe.
>
> (3.6.37)

There is, in other words, a mortality in this garden; it is a natural not a supernatural paradise. There is a permanent spring and a permanent autumn here, signifying eternal growth and the eternal harvest of that growth. The garden is an extended metaphor for a perfected natural order, containing both a cycle of birth, decay, and death, and an eternal principle of renewal.

In the center of this world is a "stately mount" reaching to the boundary of the divine world. Here reside Venus and Adonis who, in their mythic roles, elaborate the meaning of this romantic world. Venus, the perfect pattern of nature, continually enjoys Adonis, the "father of all formes" who is "by succession made perpetual". Venus' role as a personification of order, beauty, and grace is exploited in the Temple of Venus passage of Book IV; here in the garden Adonis is the most important mythic figure, subject always to mortality but eternally reborn. The regenerative process of birth, decay, and rebirth is summed up in the figure of Adonis. It is a restorative process limited to the natural world because of the dependence on the mutability of forms, yet it retains the eternal principle of constant order. It is, in other words, an image of mitigated figural reality. The world of nature is fulfilled within its own limits rather than supernaturally, yet a principle of eternal order governs that fulfillment.

This complex image of regeneration created in the Garden of Adonis gives meaning to the narratives of regeneration in love in the poem. The love wounds of various figures in the poem are "Adonis wounds", and are cured only by a harmony of the sensual and the pure in chaste love. The reconciliation of the corrupt and chaste levels of nature, which is the result of chaste love, is comparable to the harmony in the Garden of Adonis of the mutable forms and the eternal substance of nature. Taken together these two processes of regeneration define Spenser's vision of *concordia mundi*. It is a reconciliation, according to this vision, of the passionate and pure in man, and the decaying and eternal in matter.

In the Garden of Adonis the tension between eros and the soul of man is resolved by a marriage of Cupid and Psyche. The two figures, "after long troubles",

> ... now in stedfast love and happy state
> She with him lives, and hath him borne a chyld,

> Pleasure, that doth both gods and men aggrate,
> Pleasure, the daughter of Cupid and Psyche late.
>
>   (3.6.50)

The reconciliation of man and love produces a Pleasure which pleases both men and gods, a sensual pleasure redeemed of its demonic aspects. Such a union and such a concept of pleasure is the objective of Spenser's poem of love. The removal of the pain of love through the fulfillment of chaste desire stands as a metaphor of total order.

Amoret is brought up in the Garden to be a perfect example of chaste love. Scudamour's quest for the true love embodied in Amoret is presented in Spenser's allegory of love at the end of Book IV, the Temple of Venus. The painful and blissful aspects of love are reconciled in this region, sustaining and reinforcing the resolutions of love conflicts throughout the poem. Amoret's presence in the Temple equates her with both the painful and blissful sides of love, and Scudamour's conquest of Amoret constitutes his initiation into love. He speaks of his quest as a journey of peril:

> So on that hard adventure forth I went,
> And to the place of perill shortly came;
> That was a temple faire and auncient,
> Which of great mother Venus bare the name.
>
>   (4.10.5)

The Temple is "wall'd by nature gainst invaders wrong", but Scudamour begins his invasion by capturing the shield of love whose motto reads: "Blessed the man that well can use his blis: / Whose ever be the shield, faire Amoret be his". He succeeds in passing the perils of doubt, delay, and danger, and enters the region of the Temple proper where he discovers an earthly paradise of lovers:

> All these together by themselves did sport
> Their spotlesse pleasure and sweet loves content.
>
>   (4.10.26)

He approaches the Temple, which he learns is not a temple of virginity, and observes the figure of Concord, who keeps harmony between love and hate:

By her the heaven is in his course contained.
And all the world in state unmoved stands,
As their almightie maker first ordained,
And bound them with inviolable bands;
Else would the waters overflow the lands,
And fire devoure the ayre, and hell them quight,
But that she holds them with her blessed hands.
She is the nourse of pleasure and delight,
And unto Venus grace the gate doth open right.   (4.10.35)

The power of concord is extended beyond the harmony of love
and hate to the harmony of the entire natural world. Spenser
indicates that Concord "divinely grew", clearly identifying this
force as a function of the *lex aeterna* which maintains a perfect,
rational order in the world of nature. Most important for the
theme of this poem of love is the description of Concord as "the
nourse of pleasure and delight", for it provides an equation between "spotlesse pleasures and sweet loves content" and the perfect order of the natural world. In other words, chaste love and
the perfection of nature become synonymous.

This function of Concord serves as a fitting introduction to
Venus, herself a principle of order by virtue of the beauty (harmony) she represents. Her legs are entwined with a snake "whose
head and tail were fast combyned", and she is both male and
female, symbolic of a universal concord. And, to repeat a passage
already quoted, Venus with

... smyling looke doest pacifie
The raging seas, and makst the stormes to flie;
Thee, goddesse, thee the winds, the clouds doe feare,
And, when thou spredst thy mantle forth on hie,
The waters play, and pleasant lands appeare,
And heavens laugh, and al the world shews joyous cheare.
(4.10.44)

Venus may restore "pleasant lands" and tame the ragings of
nature, but she also provokes sexual desire, a necessary dimension for Spenser's double goddess, but a dimension which is
tempered by the principle of "generation":

The raging Buls rebellow through the wood,
And breaking forth dare tempt the deepest flood

To come where thou doest draw them with desire.
So all things else, that nourish vitall blood,
Soone as with fury thou doest them inspire,
In generation seeke to quench their inward fire.

                                                (4.10.46)

The power of Venus to restore to the world a pattern of divine
order is a sterile principle without the force of sexual passion
within nature. The two forces, however, are meant to harmonize.
The fallen world is restored to order by the force of Venus' beauty
or harmony, and the regenerative power of love which she in-
spires relieves the corruptions and sufferings of passion in the
ideal of chaste love and the generation of a redeemed progeny.

   In this atmosphere Scudamour reaches the object of his quest,
chaste love, or the harmony of the divine virtue of chastity and
the natural "virtue" of sensuality, embodied in Amoret. The success of this quest is a fitting conclusion to Spenser's poem of
love, for it expresses, in terms which extend beyond the personal
initiations of Scudamour and Amoret into the world of true love,
that vision of a redeemed world to which Spenser directs every
aspect of the poem.

   The Temple of Venus and the Garden of Adonis are the two
most important parts of Spenser's design in Books III and IV.
The Garden of Adonis defines a natural world perfected by a
harmony of the divine principle of eternal order and the natural
principle of generation, growth, and mutability. The Temple of
Venus defines a natural world perfected by the harmony of the
divine principle of chastity and the natural principle of sensuality.
The three love quests provide a narrative pattern of regeneration
and reconciliation, an action necessary for the imitation of the
redemption of nature. Chaste love is the objective of this pattern
of action, an objective which redeems the corruptions, the fear,
and the wounds of love, initiates the lovers into a regenerate
world of love, and maintains that redeemed world through the
generation of noble offspring. Such an objective amounts to an
imitation of nature improved by the alignment of its demands
with the virtuous pattern of the divine law.

IV. MILTON'S *COMUS*

The nature imitated in *Comus* is, like fairy land, two dimensional, and the poem's structure is made up of the conflict between these dimensions, leading to the harmony of oppositions and thus the redemption of nature. The two aspects of nature again appear in their figurative guises of passion and purity, or the lawless and the lawful. Also, a chaste heroine is at the center of this conflict between the sensual and the chaste; but unlike Books III and IV of *The Faerie Queene* there is no reunion of lovers in *Comus* – a marriage metaphor for the fulfillment of chaste love appears only in the epilogue. Although the Lady in *Comus* has no lover and thus her success in the forest cannot be compared to Britomart's initiation into love with Artegall (or to the other love unions in the poem), the journey the Lady takes through the disordered wood of nature to the *concordia* of her father's kingdom is in some ways comparable, both structurally and in intent, to the love quests of Spenser's poem. The structure of the action in both instances is, of course, that regenerative pattern which moves the characters from a condition of pain to some kind of condition of bliss or happiness. In Spenser, the anticipation caused by the pain and fear of love is resolved by a number of reconciliations of chaste love which taken together provide a complex image of harmony. And, as I have argued in the previous chapter, this image of harmony stands for the perfection of the natural world. In *Comus*, the Lady similarly enters a world of corruption and bondage, is released from that world, and restored to a condition of virtuous order in her father's kingdom. The pattern of action is the same in both cases: a movement from the corruption and disorder of sensual experience to the

purity and order of chaste innocence. The resolution of *Comus*
also provides a metaphor for an ordered nature.

The test of chastity itself, plus the content of the argument
between the Lady and Comus, relates the problem of *Comus* to
the problem of Spenser's poem of love. Britomart survives the
seduction of Malecasta and destroys the House of Busirane
through the power of chastity; the Lady counters the naturalistic
temptations of Comus with her own chaste conception of the
proper use of nature. Both of these victories are accomplished
by virtue of the heroine's chastity, plus divine aid which is due
such a virtue. The distinction between an unregenerate and regenerate nature is made in both instances; and the resolutions
of the similar conflicts between passion and purity are made by
restoring the content of nature to its rightful position in alignment
with the divine world. In this restoration, neither Britomart rejects the natural (for she accepts a chastened love), nor the Lady
(for she argues for a lawful enjoyment of nature). Both resolutions, then, serve to represent the redeemed world of nature. The
Lady's safe arrival at the court, the objective of her journey,
provides a final dramatic moment of concord and reconciliation
which replaces, and serves the same function as, the union of
lovers in Spenser's poem. Comus is driven out of nature, and the
festivities at the court celebrate the safe arrival of the chaste
heroine who is looked upon as a human or natural reflection of
universal or divine law.

Although the celebration of virtue and order at the end of
Comus provides an image of a perfected nature in the sense that
the lower level of nature (Comus) has been cast out and the
chaste daughter has been reunited with her father in his noble
and harmonious kingdom, there is in the epilogue to the poem
an image of marriage and concord which reinforces, on a more
mythic level, the order that prevails at the end of the action
proper, and which brings *Comus* into a closer relationship with
Spenser's poem. The marriage, of course, does not involve the
Lady, but its meaning reflects back upon the action of the poem
and gives it a broader range of meaning. The theme which becomes evident in *Comus* is not merely the unassailability of

chastity, but rather the proper use of nature which consists of the purification of the forces of life. Chastity functions here, as in Spenser, as a condition by which the double potential of man and nature may be harmonized into a single reality consisting of the reconciliation of the natural and the divine. The chaste heroine does not need to prove her chastity, but when that virtue becomes active in the world of nature the demonic aspects of that world are removed and the result is a nature redeemed, or realigned with the divine world. This thematic concern is sustained by the epilogue which presents an image of concord totally removed from the drama of the forest but related to it in much the same way as the mythical images of the Garden of Adonis and the Temple of Venus are related to the narrative of quest in Spenser's poem.

The earthly paradise invoked by the Attendant Spirit in the epilogue, itself a vision of a perfected nature, is the scene for this marriage between Cupid and Psyche which produces the offspring youth and joy. The purity of their union in love generates an acceptable innocent pleasure which thoroughly mitigates the effect of Comus' demonic sexuality on the world and provides the alternative image of a natural world containing a spotless harmony of the human soul and the desire of love. It is an image of a restored nature because the demands of sensual pleasure are not rejected, but purified and brought into alignment with the divine world of order and virtue. The narrative of the poem itself and the epilogue stand in complementary relationship to each other; one providing that "tension of responsibility" between the lowest and highest demands made upon man in his mediate position in the world, the other providing an image of the ideal resolution of the conflict. Although the epilogue indicates most clearly that this resolution consists of "chaste love" and therefore of the purification rather than the rejection of the forces of life, the action of the poem proper not only sets up the terms of the conflict between passion and purity, but it too suggests that nature is properly used when it is redeemed of its corrupt aspects. Like Malecasta and Busirane, Comus is rejected, but nature is not.

There are then, two images of order in *Comus* created for the purpose of expressing the perfection or redemption of nature. First, the successful arrival of the virtuous Lady at the court of her father; and second, the ideal marriage of Cupid and Psyche in the epilogue. There is very little apprehension generated concerning the ultimate success of the Lady's journey. Nevertheless, the argument with Comus and the temporary bondage serve to express the conflict between the proper and the improper use of nature, and the identity of the resolution to the confict. The reconciliation of father and daughter at the court, which is said to be a place of nobility and virtue, provides a fitting resolution to the opposition between the lustful and the pure in the action of the poem proper. The marital union of the epilogue heightens the level of poetic expression to an idealized natural scene, and has the effect of reinforcing the terms of perfection supplied in the action of the poem. This increment of meaning in *Comus* is a Spenserian touch, comparable to that extension of fairy land provided by the Garden of Adonis. The wood in *Comus*, which is often wrongly thought of as only "drear", is both a benevolent and a malign setting for the action; it is an imitation of nature in both its corrupt and ordered aspects. In contrast, the Hesperian gardens of the epilogue imitate a totally purified natural world which serves as the setting for the ideal marriage of man and desire. Such a concord creates a figure which represents the world of nature redeemed.

In spite of the similarities between *Comus* and Spenser's poem of love – the common theme of the redemption of nature, and the general pattern of action which moves from the corrupt or lawless to the pure or lawful – the two works are quite distinct from each other in the way they are organized and in the way they imitate nature. The accumulation of event and imagery in Books III and IV of *The Faerie Queene* into an elaborate design devoted to representing the primacy of concord over discord in the world is replaced in *Comus*, to a certain extent, by a more sustained causal dramatic action. The conventions of the masque, of course, limit the realism of the drama of *Comus*, and there is no cause for apprehension in the reader concerning the out-

come of the problem once it is established. The poem is, however, quite obviously organized to create an anticipation in the
reader from the very start. The tension begins with the Attendant
Spirit's declaration of mission in the natural world, and is sustained until the Lady reaches the safety and virtue of her father's
kingdom. In contrast, the epilogue is more Spenserian – supplying
an image instead of an action.

More important, however, is the difference between Spenser's
and Milton's imitation of nature. I have already suggested that
the theme of the two poems is the same, and by implication that
the two views of nature are the same – a natural world of two
dimensions, manifesting both the divine and the demonic worlds
above and below nature. The forest of *Comus*, however, is a
differently imitated nature than fairy land. Milton reveals a more
cautious introduction of the demonic and the divine into nature
than Spenser. While Spenser ranges with a high degree of poetic
boldness from the lowest to the highest levels of nature, Milton
more cautiously reduces Comus, the Spirit, Sabrina, Haemony,
etc. to the common denominator of the forest. It is a pastoral
world created to include both dimensions of nature, nature controlled by agents of the devil and nature controlled by agents of
God. This difference between fairy land and the forest may be
described in terms of Frye's theory of displacement. The forest
of *Comus*, while decidedly an imitation of nature which allows
the poetic marvelous in the form of the demonic and the divine,
is further displaced from the mythic world than fairy land, which
admits to its extensive regions dungeons, undersea caves, magic
mirrors, prophecies, sacred temples, infernal processions, and
gardens of corruption and perfection.

The landscapes of both the forest and fairy land imitate nature
in its double aspect, but in *Comus* there is a more consistent use
of irony to identify this double world. While irony is employed
by Spenser in a rather loose way, in the contrast between the
pain and bliss of love or the contrast between the image of foetal
incest and the image of a hermaphrodite union, Milton uses irony
or parody in a much more consistent fashion to define the nature
of his view of the world. By developing a conscious ambiguity in

Comus, Milton is able to reveal that nature is either demonic or divine depending on what use is made of it. Such an ambiguity is necessary for the expression of the theme under consideration here, for nature is not to be rejected, but simply purified of what is demonic in it. The ironic similarity between Comus' revels and the final dance at court, the pastoral disguise of both Comus and the Attendant Spirit, and Comus' assertion that he imitates the "starry quire", are all examples of Milton's technique of establishing a double, and reversible, view of the world of nature. It is appropriate now to look at the poem more closely.

In the first passage of the poem the Attendant Spirit describes his descent into the world, or more precisely the transfer of his "immortal shape" from a celestial order to the realm of fallen nature, in terms of a contrast between the "serene Ayr" of the higher regions and the "smoak and stirr" of the earth. The region from where he comes ("before the starry threshold of *Joves* Court") is not the totally divine world, but rather the limit of the created universe which exists at the threshold of the eternally divine world. He becomes, so to speak, naturalized, for he leaves the purity and serenity of the highest level of nature to enter that level of nature which is the ground for the conflict between the sensual and the pure. In addition, the Spirit indicates the general contrast on which the poem is based: There are men on earth who are "Unmindful of the crown that virtue gives", yet there are some who "by due steps aspire / To lay their just hands on that Golden Key / That ope's the Palace of Eternity". It is only for this latter kind of person, he asserts, that he would soil his purity with the "rank vapours" of the earth. Specifically, he has come to earth to protect the Lady and her two brothers, who are "fair off-spring nurs't in Princely lore". This protection is necessary, for the young people are passing through a "drear wood",

> The nodding horror of whose shady brows
> Threats the forlorn and weary Passinger.[1]

The characterization here of the wood as dreary and threatening is contradicted as well as supported through the poem. The Lady

---

[1] Ll. 38-9. All references to *Comus* are from *The Student's Milton*, ed. F. A. Patterson (New York, 1933).

speaks of it as "hospitable" as well as "tangl'd". The imagery surrounding the brothers and their berry picking is certainly not suggestive of a dreary wood; and the Spirit himself, after his pastoral transformation into Thyrsis, indulges in a "pleasing fit of melancholy" in the wood "to meditate my rural minstrelsie" (545-6). The images used to describe the wood do not have as their source any single absolute quality. The wood changes from benevolent to threatening, or is both at once, depending on what level of nature is being expressed through it. This shifting meaning of the forest in the poem indicates the different values which can be derived from nature. The wild and tangled wood is a figure for Comus' use of nature to pervert and imbrute, while the hospitable, peaceful wood is a figure for nature in conformity with universal law.

The Spirit continues with a vivid description of Comus, his origin, and his influence. He is descended from

> Bacchus that first from out the purple Grape,
> Crush't the sweet poyson of mis-used Wine.
>
> (46-7)

The metaphor of mis-used wine in this passage not only expresses the improper or naturalistic activities of Bacchus (and through him, Comus), but it also implies that wine need not be mis-used. If the improper use of wine can serve as a metaphor for the improper use of nature, then the suggestion that wine may be properly used supplies an important clue to the ambiguous view of nature in the poem: depending on the use of nature by man, the world is corrupting or ennobling. The proper use of nature is, of course, that use which conforms to the requirements of the *lex aeterna*.

In addition, the Bacchus passage introduces the motif of cup and liquor which is used in different ways throughout the poem. The cup of Comus' mother, Circe, is an elaboration of this motif:

> . . . who knows not *Circe*
> The daughter of the Sun? Whose charmed Cup
> Whoever tasted, lost his upright shape,
> And downward fell into a groveling Swine.
>
> (50-53)

In the same manner, Comus

> Excells his mother at her mighty Art,
> Offring the every weary Travailer,
> His orient liquor in a Crystal Glasse . . . .
> Soon as the Potion works, their human count'nance,
> Th' express resemblance of the gods, is chang'd
> Into som brutish form of Woolf, or Bear,
> Or Ounce, or Tiger, Hog, or bearded Goat.
>
> (63-65; 68-71)

The two levels of nature are indicated here through the double potential in bi-form man to resemble either the gods or the brutes. The corruption of man by surrendering to the demonic in nature is expressed by the drinking of the "orient liquor". The effects of this cup are a demonic parody of the effects of the cup of such a figure as Spenser's Cambine, who creates a concord between Triamond and Cambell with her drink of Nepenthe. While Comus' cup imbrutes, Cambine's drink is said to precede the divinization of man. In *Comus*, the ironic comparison between drinks that transform is apparent in the similarity of Comus' brutish wine and the liquid from a "fountain pure" with which Sabrina frees the Lady from her stony bondage.

This first passage of the poem concludes with the Spirit putting off his "skie robes" and completing the transformation from immortal to mortal shape by taking on the likeness of a pastoral swain:

> Who with his soft Pipe, and smooth-dittied Song,
> Well knows to still the wilde winds when they roar,
> And hush the waving Woods . . .
>
> (86-88)

The Spirit thus claims for himself the power of orphic song by which he will be able to introduce a moral harmony to the corruptions of the drear wood controlled by Comus, the effect of which will be to guide the Lady safely through this level of nature (the claim of course turns out to be somewhat presumptuous, for Thyrsis must resort eventually to the powers of Haemony and Sabrina). The whole passage (1-92) introduces, in the person of Thyrsis, the influence of that ordered part of the created universe which lies on the boundary between the world of nature and the world of spirit. This influence becomes, poetically, part of the world of fallen nature, and reinforces the power of the Lady's chastity. The scene of the action of the poem is, then, a region which reveals the demonic working within nature (Comus) and the divine working within nature (Thyrsis, and in a more human way, the Lady herself). The action itself is the conflict between these forces, and the subsequent cleansing of nature of the influence of the demonic.

Comus enters the poem with a description of his activities and an expression of faith in them. In position and general intention, this passage is derived from the "anti-masque" of Jonson. However, it not only serves as a contrast to Thyrsis and his virtuous mission, but it also develops those aspects of Comus' activities which ironically imitate or parody the virtuous forces within and around the Lady. There is, first of all, the distinction between night and day. The day for Comus is equated with sin; but for Thyrsis, the Lady, and her brothers, sin is associated with night. When Comus states that "Tis onely day-light that makes Sin", he means that only when one is under the clarity, the reason of day is there such a concept as sin. It is the purity and divinity of reason which defines the impurity of its lack. When the Elder Brother calls upon the moon and the stars to "disinherit Chaos, that raigns here", he expresses the belief that the "Stygian darknes" of Comus' revelry is unquestionably a perversion, a beclouding of the light of reason and virtue.

Within this hellish darkness, however, there is a ritual of dancing and mirth which serves as an ironic parallel to the "rural dance" and the "mirth and chere" of all the pastoral swains at the end of the poem. In addition, the activities of Comus' herd expressed in lines such as "Braid your locks with rosie Twine / Dropping odours, dropping Wine", are recalled in Thyrsis' description of Sabrina:

> And gave her to his daughters to imbathe
> In nectar'd lavers strew'd with Asphodil,
> And through the porch and inlet of each sense
> Dropt in Ambrosial Oils till she reviv'd.
>
>   (836-39)

> ... and oft at Eave
> Visits the herds along the twilight meadows,
> Helping all urchin blasts, and ill luck signes
> That the shrewd medling Elfe delights to make,
> Which she with pretious viold liquors heals.

(842-46)

A floral world is invoked in both instances, but it is quite clear that Comus has a corrupting influence upon his herd, while Sabrina has a redemptive influence upon hers. This double use of the imagery of the natural world allows Milton to distinguish between "diverse laws" of nature rather than to replace the natural world with a transcendent order of virtue.

The most explicit indication of this irony is given by Comus himself:

> We that are of purer fire
> Imitate the Starry Quire.

(111-12)

Like Cupid who claims to replace Jove, and Satan who takes evil to be his good, Comus asserts that his power replaces the influence of the spherical harmony in the world. Such evidence indicates that Milton does not merely express the opposition of two sets of values in the world of nature; he shows that they are also reversible: the demonic parodies the divine, or the hellish serves as an ironic counterpart to the heavenly in nature. The ironic relationship created between the forces of good and evil suggests that the state of man in nature is a condition with a potential in either direction. As Woodhouse states, "the beauty which is to the good a good is the same beauty which the evil pervert to evil ends".[2] The world of nature is fundamentally innocent (as the Lady herself asserts); it may be properly or improperly used.

The virgin Lady's approach causes Comus to break off the debauchery of the dark wood. In order to more easily tempt the Lady into his herd and to drink from his cup, Comus hurls a spell into the "spungy ayr" which dissolves the scene of revelry

---

[2] A. S. P. Woodhouse, "The Argument of Milton's *Comus*", *University of Toronto Quarterly*, XI (1948), p. 63.

and transforms him into "some harmles Villager". Comus' spell
removes the appearance of the demonic from the scene and
changes it to an illusion of pastoral benevolence. In this disguise
Comus later attempts to persuade the Lady to drink from his
cup and to enjoy the bounty of nature. Just as his figure is an
illusion of pastoral virtue, his argument is an illusion of rationality
and rightness.

The Lady enters the scene reflecting on the now silenced noises
of Comus' revelry:

> . . . the sound
> Of Riot, and ill manag'd Merriment,
> Such as the jocund Flute, or gamesome Pipe
> Stirs up among the loose unletter'd Hinds,
> When for the teeming Flocks, and granges full
> In wanton dance they praise the bounteous Pan,
> And thank the gods amiss . . .
>
> (170-76)

The ill-managed merriment and the wrongful praise of the gods
is clearly a variation of the mis-use of wine spoken of earlier in
the poem. The sounds of this music are associated with irration-
ality, perverse worship, and wantonness; but again there is an
implication that music need not be related to evil. Thyrsis himself intends to still the wild and waving wood with pipe and song.

In continuing her reflections, the Lady refers to the forest in
two different ways:

> . . . O where els
> Shall I inform my unacquainted feet
> In the blind mazes of this tangl'd Wood?
> My brothers when they saw me wearied out
> With this long way, resolving here to lodge
> Under the spreading favor of these Pines,
> Stept as they se'd to the next Thicket side
> To bring me berries, or such cooling fruit
> As the kind hospitable woods provide.
>
> (178-86)

The forest is, significantly, chaotic around Comus and benevolent
around the Lady and her brothers before their separation. The
night has come, the stars have been closed up; it can only forbode

"som fellonious end", and the Lady is plagued with fearful fantasies. Abruptly her mood changes to one of firm confidence in her virtuous mind and body. She sees visibly the "unblemish't form of Chastity" as a silver gleam is cast over the grove. With her spirits thus "enliv'nd" she sings a song to attract the attention of her brothers. The beauty of this song, which turns out to be an appeal to the "unseen" nymph, Echo, for assistance, deeply affects Thyrsis who is, we later discover, nearby. He tells of hearing the song after the "barbarous dissonance" of Comus' revelry:

> At last a soft and solemn breathing sound
> Rose like a steam of rich distill'd Perfumes.
>
> (554-55)

The presence of the divine in the world of nature is expressed by the silver gleam of chastity, the virtue of the Lady herself, and the palpable beauty of her song. Comus, too, is affected by the song. He recognizes that its beauty identifies the Lady as an earthly agent of the divine world:

> Can any mortal mixture of the Earths mould
> Breath such Divine inchanting ravishment?
> Sure something holy lodges in that breast,
> And with these raptures moves the vocal air
> To testify his hidd'n residence.
>
> (243-47)

He makes a comparison between the enchantment of the Lady's song and the enchantment of the herbs and drugs of Circe, concluding that these drugs "lull'd the sense" and "rob'd it of it self", while the Lady arouses one to delight and bliss. He goes on to say that a "forren wonder" such as this lady could only have her origin in the "blest Song" of the "Goddes . . . in rurall shrine" which forbids "every bleak unkindly Fog / To touch the prosperous growth of this tall Wood". In his reaction to the song Comus seems to drop out of character; it appears that Milton has made a rather gratuitous and certainly undeveloped suggestion that the demonic aspect of nature is susceptible to the redemptive powers of the divine world revealed in a human agent. The suggestion is undeveloped because the poem ends with the re-

jection of Comus rather than his inclusion in the final festivities
of concord. Only at this one point does he seem to be in danger
of succumbing to the Lady's own spell.[3]

Following Comus' reaction to the song, he and the Lady speak
for the first time. Comus pretends to allay the Lady's fear of the
"dim darknes, and this leavy Labyrinth" by promising to lead
her to a "low but loyal cottage". He describes this illusion of
protection in terms of pastoral serenity: "bosky bourne", "low-
roosted lark", and "thatch't pallat". The Lady's agreement to be
led off by a figure of evil appearing good sustains Milton's purpose to portray an ambiguous nature in which the demonic has
an ironic semblance to the virtuous. At this point in the developing action of the poem the common denominator of the pastoral world includes not only the journey of the Lady and her
brothers, but Comus and Thyrsis as well. The brothers seek their
sister in the forest, the Lady follows the false swain Comus to a
rustic cottage, and Thyrsis, another kind of "false" swain, attends
the destiny of the young travelers.

The scene shifts at this point to the two brothers. The forest
is compared to a state of chaos by the Elder Brother, and he
appeals to the celestial regions of the created universe to remove
this condition of disorder:

> Unmuffle ye faint stars, and thou fair Moon
> That wontst to love the travailers benizon,
> Stoop thy pale visage through an amber cloud,
> And disinherit *Chaos*, that raigns here
> In double night of darknes, and of shades . . .
>
> (330-34)

And if this redeeming influence "be quite damm'd up with black
usurping mists":

---

[3] The driving-off of Comus into the forest is just as effective in creating
a metaphor for the cleansing of nature as the total destruction of Comus
would be. Busirane is permanently removed from fairy land, and Parolles,
in *All's Well*, is allowed to join the final festivities after his demonic
powers are rendered ineffectual. The effect is the same in both cases.
Between these extremes of complete destruction and readmittance into
society falls the fate of Comus, who is driven off but remains potentially
dangerous. This kind of defeat of Comus is consistent, perhaps, with the
fact that Milton's poem is less "romantic" than Spenser's, but more
"romantic" than Shakespeare's.

> ... a rush Candle from the wicker hole
> Of som clay habitation visit us
> With thy long levell'd rule of streaming light,
> And thou shalt be our star of Arcady.
>
> (337-40)

The restorative powers of the celestial region may be replaced
by the similar powers of the pastoral world, indicating a commerce between the purity of the realm of spheres and the purity
of a pastoralized world. The downward progression from a higher
to a lower order of perfection is completed by the Elder Brother's
assertion that

> Vertue could see to do what vertue would
> By her own radiant light, though Sun and Moon
> Were in the flat Sea sunk.
>
> (372-74)

The power of light to disinherit chaos has passed from the celestial star to the Arcadian candle, and finally to the radiance of
chastity itself. The fact that Milton associates the power of chastity with the other redemptive powers suggests that the thematic
interest in *Comus* extends beyond the unassailable passage of
the chaste through the world of temptation to a kingdom of
nobility and virtue. The image of chastity here as a restorative
power provides that link between the worlds of nature and spirit
which is necessary for imitating a natural world perfected by
virtue of its conformity to the content of the world of spirit. The
beauty and chastity of the Lady are qualities which conform to
the content of the divine world, and they are capable of removing
disorder from the world of nature. Chastity serves in *Comus,*
then, to represent that level of nature which is in accord with the
universal law. The meaning of this image of purity extends to
the condition of physical nature as well as to the moral condition
of man.

> ... beauty like the fair Hesperian Tree
> Laden with blooming gold, had need the guard
> Of dragon watch with uninchanted eye,
> To save her blossoms, and defend her fruit
> From the rash hand of bold Incontinence.
>
> (392-96)

Here the ideal purity of the Lady is compared to a condition of earthly paradise, expressed by the golden apples of the Hesperian tree. The drama of the Lady's passage through the wood does not only establish chastity as an image of moral perfection because of its commerce with the divine world, but it also increasingly enlarges that image to include the perfection of all nature.

The brothers fail to agree, however, on whether chastity is indeed sufficiently strong to protect itself, or whether some additional aid is required:

> *Eld. Bro.* My sister is not so defenceless left
> As you imagine, she has a hidden strength
> Which you remember not.
>
> *2. Bro.* What hidden strength,
> Unless the strength of Heav'n, if you mean that?
>
> *Eld. Bro.* I mean that too, but yet a hidden strength
> Which if Heav'n gave it, may be term'd her own.
>
> (413-18)

The harmonious conclusion that chastity is both a personal strength and a divine gift satisfies the conditions that man has the capacity to redeem himself but that his redemptive power carries the impress of heaven. The familiar lines on chastity spoken at this point by the Elder Brother suggest a relationship between nature and spirit which gives meaning to much of the imagery of the poem:

> So dear to Heav'n is Saintly chastity,
> That when a soul is found sincerely so,
> A thousand liveried Angels lacky her,
> Driving far off each thing of sin and guilt,
> And in cleer dream and solemn vision
> Tell her of things that no gross ear can hear,
> Till oft convers with heav'nly habitants
> Begin to cast a beam on th' outward shape,
> The unpolluted Temple of the Mind,
> And turns it by degrees to the souls essence,
> Till all be made immortal . . .
>
> (452-62)

The commerce between earth and heaven, the most important structural principle in the poem because it defines that necessary conformity of nature to the divine law, is expressed in these lines. Specifically, a transformation from the mortal to the immortal is said to occur because of the effect of the divine upon the chaste soul. Such a transformation expresses the ideal perfection of the body consisting of a condition in which the effects of heaven are fully realized in an earthly agent. The harmonious interaction of the natural and the spiritual signified by this transformation is sustained by metamorphoses which occur within the action of *Comus*. The Attendant Spirit's "mortalization" to a pastoral swain is a reverse process, but it expresses the same relationship of two levels of reality. Sabrina, too, undergoes a "quick immortal change" from earthly virgin to goddess, a transformation which is a more extreme (or less displaced) version of the Elder Brother's observation of the same possibility for the Lady. The poem also includes similar transformations of the physical scene: the silver gleam, comparable to the beam referred to in the brother's speech, cast over the grove is chastity made palpable; and the Lady's song, too, has a visible effect upon nature. All of these alterations of the natural world – both humanly and elementally – attest to the "hidd'n residence" of the divine within the earthly. The poetic creation of this kind of relationship between nature and spirit is, of course, necessary for the imitation of a natural world restored to its proper position in alignment with the divine.

Thyrsis re-enters the scene and stresses the very real power Comus has for "unmoulding reasons mintage", and that this power cannot be overcome without some supernatural aid. The Haemony root is produced by Thyrsis for this purpose; it is described as having a double nature. In the pastoral forest it is darkish and has prickles on it; in "another Countrey" it bears a "bright golden flowre". This root is another example of the expression of the separation but interaction of the earthly and the heavenly. It has its full, ideal flowering in a heavenly order, yet even on earth it can produce "divine effect".

Deep in the woods the Lady sits in an enchanted chair, confronted by Comus and his rabble. He has turned to alabaster the Lady's "corporal rinde"; but the divine quality of her virginity, the freedom of her mind to be chaste, is not affected. The argument with which Comus attempts to sway the mind of the Lady emphasizes the unnaturalness and wastefulness of her virgin condition. He accuses her of inverting the covenant of nature's trust, and dealing

> . . . . like an ill borrower
> With that which you receiv'd on other terms,
> Scorning the unexempt condition
> By which all mortal frailty must subsist.
>
> (682-85)

The argument, of course, is in the tradition of naturalism. Within the context of the poem Comus' invocation of a covenant or a "law" of nature functions in the same ironic way as the rest of his activities. It is a demonic parody of that law of nature derived from the *lex aeterna*, and which includes in its statutes the rightness of chastity. The unnatural to Comus is the Stoic "lean and sallow Abstinance", the wasting of the vitality of nature. For the Lady the unnatural is the "mis-used wine", the "ill manag'd merriment", or any use of nature which excludes the government of the natural law. She speaks of "most innocent nature" who "Means her provision onely to the good / That live according to her sober law". The "Sun-clad power of chastity" is clearly a fulfillment of these sober laws, and it is this doctrine which the Lady accuses Comus of not understanding.

Although she rejects the naturalistic argument of Comus, the Lady does not reject nature itself. She believes, as Comus does, that the provisions of nature should not be wasted, that "natural felicity" (of which Sidney speaks) should not be renounced. It is clear that for her, chastity and the proper use of nature are equated; she does not identify chastity with the total renunciation of the natural felicity of the body. Chastity serves in the poem as a representation of the natural law, which includes in its government the proper use of rather than the renunciation of the sensual forces of nature. Chastity, then, functions in *Comus*, as chaste love does in Spenser's poem of love, as a metaphor for a perfected or redeemed natural world. It has, like chaste love, a range of meaning beyond the personal quality of the Lady herself. The extensive restorative power of this poetically heightened virtue is suggested by the Lady when she states that it would be possible for "the uncontrouled worth / Of this pure cause" to

> . . . kindle my rap't spirits
> To such a flame of sacred vehemence,
> That dumb things would be mov'd to sympathize,
> And the brute Earth would lend her nerves, and shake
> Till all thy magick structures rear'd so high,
> Were shatter'd into heaps o're thy false head.
>
> (793-98)

Milton's emphasis on the independent sufficiency of the human condition of chastity throughout the poem is rather disappointingly fulfilled. Although the Lady does not succumb to Comus' temptations at the end, she does allow herself to be led off by him and emprisoned, only to be released by external means. Milton's failure to demonstrate very firmly the independent power of chastity may be taken as a weakness in the poem. On the other hand, it is important for his conception of the relationship between the earthly and the divine that human virtue be seen as a function of a higher order ("a hidden strength / Which if Heav'n gave it, may be termed her own"), and must wait upon heaven for its complete activation. In addition, the mode of representation to which Milton commits himself limits the power that such a human heroine as the Lady can have. She is poetically humanized, but Comus is not, which seems to disallow her from fighting him altogether on his own terms. Milton apparently is aware of the problem, for he continually suggests characteristics of the Lady which are not really hers at all. In addition to her unfulfilled assertion that she could destroy Comus and his herd, the Elder Brother's speech on the transformation of mortal to immortal is never literally relevant to the Lady herself. Both passages do, however, give meaning to the conception of chastity developed in the poem, even if the Lady never destroys Comus or never turns into the soul's essence. The more romantic (or less displaced) mode of Spenser's representation allows Britomart,

for example, to counter the demonic more directly on its own
supernatural terms.

At the end of the action of the poem, Comus is removed from
the scene very abruptly. The two brothers rush in, break the
enchanted cup, and drive him off with his rabble. He does man-
age to keep his wand, the reversal of which is said to be able to
free the Lady from her stony bondage. The backward muttering
of Comus' "dissevering power" to release the Lady is consistent
with Comus' role as a demonic imitator of a higher order of
nature. What has put the Lady in bondage may also free her, if
its values are reversed. The wand, however, cannot be used; this
allows Thyrsis to call upon Sabrina for aid. Sabrina, like Thyrsis,
serves as a link between nature and the attendant powers of a
higher order. She was first human and then a goddess; she still
retains her "maid'n gentleness". Her healing power is the power
of chastity, and thus she manifests that higher aid due someone
as pure as the Lady. In addition, she is a supernatural counterpart
to the Lady. As I have already suggested, the characterization
of the Lady is not "romantic" enough to carry that weight of
chastity as an eternal essence (which Sabrina introduces). The
natural and temporal purity of the Lady is complemented by the
lasting principle of chastity represented by the goddess Sabrina.
The restoration of the Lady by Sabrina is a symbolic act indicating the dissolution of the demonic forces in nature capable
of restraining a proper commerce between earth and heaven.
This restoration is followed by the final reconciliation of the
Lady with her father and his noble court, a region in nature
untouched by the corruption of Comus.

In the epilogue, Thyrsis describes his return to the Hesperian
gardens, that idealized nature where an eternal summer prevails.
He progresses, in his description, from Hesperus to an even
higher level of nature, where the union of Cupid and Psyche
occurs. Although it is a concord of the soul and a celestial Cupid,
the region in which it takes place is not poetically represented as
beyond the limits of the range of the natural world. A union of
the psyche and divine love would hardly produce any offspring,
much less youth and joy. It is, rather, to be taken as a further

heightening of Milton's conception of the order which informs
the created universe. If the Elder Brother's central speech on
chastity were to be fulfilled, the outcome would be a figure such
as Psyche, the "souls essence", who is here the immortal principle
of purity. The reference to Psyche's "wandring labors long" as-
sociate her with the Lady in much the same way as Sabrina and
the Lady are associated. While the Lady is not able to represent
the most idealized conception of purity, Sabrina and Psyche are.
In the same way, celestial Cupid is a representation of the most
idealized conception of sensual love, an aspect of the natural
world Milton introduces here for the first time. The union of
these two principles, which is imaged in a most rarified atmosphere, produces offspring which attest to Milton's interest in
retaining the pleasures of sensuality as well as the purity of innocence.

Milton presents a hierarchy of images in *Comus*, all of which
refer to the created universe and not beyond it, and which progressively heighten the meaning of the natural world in the poem.
The movement is from the fallen world of the forest where the
corrupt and the pure contend, to the kingdom of the Lady's
father which is permanently virtuous, and then to the earthly
paradise of the Hesperian gardens

> Where young *Adonis* oft reposes,
> Waxing well of his deep wound
> In slumber soft, and on the ground
> Sadly sits th' *Assyrian* Queen.
>
> (998-1001)

From this region of eternal summer where Venus grieves and
Adonis is wounded, Milton passes to the most rarified level on
which a reconciliation of passion and purity can be made. The
natural world appears to have been left far behind, but it has
only been drained poetically of everything but the idealized
figures of love and the soul. The bothersome last few lines of
the poem do not, as often supposed, introduce a new and even
higher order. In fact, no level of the universe is imitated here at
all – as in the rest of the epilogue. There is, simply, an assertion

that virtue "can teach ye how to clime / Higher then the Spheary chime", repeating an emphasis of the entire poem: chastity aligns man with the divine world. The ascent into that world is not made in the poem itself, or is it made in these last lines. In addition, the second assertion – that heaven would stoop to aid feeble virtue – has been dramatized throughout the poem, and does not introduce here a new set of circumstances. The entire fictional world of *Comus* is devoted to indicating that a perfected natural world is a world which conforms morally and elementally to the eternal order of the divine, but is not itself divine.

In *Comus*, Milton imitates nature both as a scene of confict and a scene of interaction between contradictory levels of experience. Two different laws of nature have influence in the poem. The law of Comus, "pranckt in reasons garb", reveals that dimension of nature which is analogous to the eternally divine world of purity and order. The *concordia mundi*, or the alignment of the natural with the divine, is expressed by the successful journey of the Lady through the forest, and by the epilogue. Although Milton imitates nature in its diverse laws, and resolves the conflict by providing a metaphor for a redeemed rather than renounced nature, he is less interested than Spenser in promoting the values of natural felicity through love. The harmony of passion and purity which is established on a more thoroughly human basis in Books III and IV of *The Faerie Queene*, is relegated, in *Comus*, to the refined atmosphere of the union of Cupid and Psyche. In presenting his vision of a redeemed nature which everywhere manifests the values of a higher order, Milton's emphasis falls more on that higher order than on nature itself.

In spite of Milton's poetic technique of constantly refining the content of the natural world to the point where it is just distinguishable from the divine world, the action of the poem is grounded in nature, and it is clear that the thematic interest is the proper vs. the improper use of nature. The proper use of nature constitutes its redemption, and it is chastity which signifies this proper use. Chastity, in *Comus*, is an extensive metaphor in which is accumulated the identity of a natural world aligned with eternal order. The poem comes to this conclusion not only by providing a heightened image of chastity through the complementary figures of the Lady, Sabrina, and Psyche, but also by the drama in the forest through which the contending forces within nature are represented.

V. SHAKESPEARE'S *ALL'S WELL THAT ENDS WELL*

The term "romantic" as a description of a mode of poetic imitation has been used in this study to measure the degree to which a fictional world represents the supernatural and subnatural worlds of the divine and the demonic. Frye's theory of displacement, which is a useful way of distinguishing poetic modes of imitation, has been employed to indicate a difference between Spenser's fairy land and Milton's forest. Fairy land is relatively closer to the prototypal mode in Frye's scheme (the mythic) than is Milton's forest. Its regions allow a somewhat more direct representation of the unnatural than the world of *Comus*. Both fictional worlds are, however, displaced from the mythic mode to the degree that the limits of the natural world are never exceeded, and that the demonic and the divine function within those limits in figurative ways.

The fictional world of *All's Well That Ends Well* is further removed from the mythic than either *Comus* or Books III and IV of *The Faerie Queene*. The final three chapters have been arranged to conclude with Shakespeare's play in order to draw attention to the progressive displacement of the mythic mode of representation in these three works. It is not the intention here to generalize on the historical development of the representation of reality in Renaissance poetry, but it can be suggested that these three poems exemplify a progressive movement away from the romantic mode in the direction of the more mimetic modes, in spite of the insufficient evidence and the fact that the argument violates chronology in placing Milton between Spenser and Shakespeare.

If *Comus* is thought of as a moderate poetic reversion to the Spenserian mode, a progressive movement is recognizable in these poems toward a more circumspect and allusive way of imitating those eternal worlds of the demonic and divine which surround nature. The facility with which Spenser employs the most extreme kind of poetic marvelous, and the ease with which the special realms of such mythic figures as Venus and Adonis are introduced, is replaced in *Comus* by an extremely careful reduction of unnatural figures such as the Spirit, Comus, and Sabrina to the common ground of the pastoral forest. With the exception of the epilogue, *Comus* reveals a much more self-conscious attitude toward the representation of the supernatural through the use of the poetic marvelous than does Spenser's poem of love.

Both poems, however, imitate the demonic and divine within nature in a most direct and romantic way compared to *All's Well That Ends Well*. Shakespeare's play has the same thematic interest as the other poems, and thus presents a fictional nature of two dimensions, pulled down by the influence of the demonic world and pulled up by the influence of the divine world. But in *All's Well* instead of the tortuous regions of the House of Busirane or the enchantments of Comus, we find the more human figure of Parolles; instead of the great civil restoration in Tudor monarchy, or the refined concord of Cupid and Psyche, we find the more limited and "realistic" restoration of the Court of France and the noble birthline of Rousillon; and instead of the heroical chastity of Britomart or the rarified purity of the Lady, we find the more personalized virtue of Helena. Parolles, however, has the same demonic function as Busirane and Comus as a corruptor of nature; the restoration of the Court of France and the Rousillon birthline serves as the same kind of image of concord as the civil regeneration in Spenser's poem; and Helena, like Britomart and the Lady, is a chaste heroine whose dramatic problem represents the conflict within nature between the sensuous and the pure, and whose chastity clearly relates her to the divine world. *All's Well*, in other words, although imitating a two-dimensional nature and the influence of the eternal worlds of the demonic and the divine, reveals the presence within nature of the subnatural and super-natural in a less romantic (or more mimetic, in Frye's scheme) mode of representation than Spenser's or Milton's poem.

In addition to these differences in the way the fourfold universe is expressed in the three poems, there are interesting differences in the way Spenser, Milton, and Shakespeare approach the poetic function of love. In Books III and IV of *The Faerie Queene*, the value of the concord of chaste love for the personal lives of the characters involved is poetically heightened by "sacramentalizing" the image of this pure love until it becomes a principle of order for the entire natural world. The image of chaste love is "sacramental" not in the sense that it contains any spiritual grace, but because the meaning of the personal harmony of passion and purity is extended to include all of nature in order that the perfection of that world may be expressed.

In *Comus*, Milton employs an image of chastity as well as an image of chaste love in order to express the content of a nature which conforms to the government of the divine law. The image of chaste love in the union of Cupid and Psyche, however, appears only in the epilogue; the action of the poem itself defines the conflict of the sensual and the pure, and indicates that the virtue of chastity constitutes a proper use of nature, or a proper commerce between nature and spirit. The emphasis in *Comus* falls on the moral capacity of man living in a divided world to choose either an alignment with the devil or with God, and on the necessity for accomplishing the latter. Spenser, on the other hand, is less interested in the moral imperatives of the conduct of his characters than he is in the portrayal of a totally cleansed natural world, both morally and elementally.

In *All's Well*, Shakespeare's objective, like Spenser's, is to unite his main characters in a concord of chaste love; and, like the unions in both Spenser and Milton, the reconciliation of Bertram and Helena stands for a more inclusive order. But in *All's Well*, the interest centers less on the immense harmony of all of nature or on the general moral responsibility of man, and more on the immediate and intimate problems of life facing Helena and Bertram. We are less interested in Spenser's love quests for their dramatization of the problems of love than for the total view of nature which they represent; and we are less interested in the Lady as a person than in the moral "tension of responsibility" she signifies, or in the metaphorical function of chastity in the poem. But in *All's Well*, the drama of Helena's quest for the love of Bertram, and the drama of Bertram's progress from profligacy to virtue are the centers of interest, although the final order of true love, a renewed court, and a fulfilled birthright serves as a metaphor for the restoration of the world.

The three works have been distinguished in this manner only to suggest that the Renaissance theme of the redemption of nature is expressed in a progressively more realistic manner. The world of spells and enchantments and relatively overt mythic overtones becomes more and more difficult to sustain, and is replaced by more thoroughly human forces and figures to accomplish similar ends. The theme of redemption itself may undergo certain significant historical alterations, but it is the main intention here simply to draw attention to three different ways of imitating a similar vision of a redeemed natural world.

All's Well That Ends Well begins in disorder and ends in order. At the very start of the play we discover a number of factors that have contributed to the disintegration of both love and society. The former Count of Rousillon is dead (and the great tradition of virtue and nobility with him), leaving Bertram, the new Count, fatherless, and his mother, the Countess, husbandless. Helena's father, a physician who possessed remarkable healing powers, is also dead. The King of France is suffering from a fistula; and the Florentines are in need of French aid in their war. From a more romantic perspective, Helena, the heir to much of her father's powers and the possessor of some mysterious power of her own, finds herself in love with Bertram, and is unable at first to find a way to circumvent or destroy the social as well as the emotional barrier between them. And Bertram, heir to the noble line of Rousillon, seems to promise very little beside his handsome figure for the fulfillment of his noble birthright. These circumstances, made clear at the outset, define a society of youth in which both Helena and Bertram have particular destinies to fulfill: Helena must reconcile her conflict of desire and fear of love, and establish a rightful union with Bertram; Bertram must renounce his profligate ways and become fit to bear the name of Rousillon. The older society is represented primarily by the Countess, who in spite of her tie to the past understands the problem of the young Helena and aids her in solving it. In addition to an unrequited love and an unfulfilled birthright, the King of France requires a cure for his fistula (symbolic of the restoration of the whole diseased court). These are the objectives of the action; and it is quite plain that these objectives involve social integration as well as personal concord. With this background in mind it is possible to separate three related patterns of actions in the play which all contribute to the central theme and are restorative in effect: initiation, purification, and death and revival.

The restorative action of initiation involves both Helena and Bertram. In both cases the content of the life of the character is transformed. The progress of the initiation is, however, different in each instance. Helena with great determination embarks on her purposeful quest for the love of Bertram; while Bertram is until the very last unwilling to acknowledge the change that is taking place in his life. An observation in Mircea Eliade's *Birth and Rebirth* briefly identifies the nature of Helena's initiation:

> . . . the pre-eminent religious experience of woman is that of the sanctity of life and the mystery of child-bearing and universal fecundity. . . . woman's initiation par excellence is her introduction to the mystery of generation, primordial symbol of spiritual regeneration.[1]

Helena is faced with the problem of fulfilling herself as a women through her love for Bertram, which of course must be returned. This problem takes dramatic form in the play in the conflict between sensual passion and virginal purity. Helena both desires and fears the transformation from maid to woman. She recognizes that the initiation into womanhood can be accomplished only by a submission to sensuality, but she is determined that the submission shall not qualify the ultimate value of her chastity.

---

[1] (New York, 1958), p. 80.

This conflict is introduced in the first scene of the play. Parolles and Helena are engaged in a discussion of virginity. Consistent with her status as a young virgin, Helena exclaims, "Man is enemy to virginity; how may we barricado it against him?" Parolles is not at all sympathetic with Helena's position, and much like Comus he argues that "it is not politic in the commonwealth of nature to preserve virginity. Loss of virginity is rational increase, and there was never virgin got till virginity was first lost." He insists that virginity violates the "rule of nature", and finally Helena is forced to reveal an attitude toward her viginity which seems to be related to her desire for Bertram: "How might one do, sir, to lose it to her own liking?" This means, of course, to accept the demands of passion but not to surrender the virtue of chastity. It is a compromise which is important to each one of the poems discussed in these chapters. It recalls Spenser's chaste desire and Milton's spotless union. Its significance is in the fact that it represents the harmony of Venus and Diana, passion and purity; and that the reconciliation of the conflicting dimensions of nature results in the chastening rather than the renunciation of the drives of life. At the end of the argument with Parolles, Helena vows that she will continue to preserve her virginity, but the problem of her life has been established: how to fulfill her passion for Bertram without subverting her virtue of chastity. In addition, the argument introduces to the play the demonic function of Parolles, who is committed to the "naturalistic" or libertine point of view. His "rule of nature" echoes Comus' "covenant of Nature"; they both invoke a false "law" of nature in that they both reject those chaste demands upon man which align him and his world with the universal order. Parolles expresses his position to Helena in his statement that he hopes that "my instruction shall serve to naturalize thee", by which he means that he hopes he can convince Helena of the "naturalness" of sex. In spite of the correlation between this hope and the obvious destiny of Helena, Parolles' "naturalness" is a demonic counterpart to the naturalness Helena seeks; it is entirely devoid of any commitment to the government of the divine law, and is thus unacceptabe to the chaste heroine.

The conflict between passion and purity is continued throughout the play up to the point when the marriage of Helena and Bertram is finally consummated with the aid of the Florentine maid, Diana. Bertram's mother, the Countess of Rousillon, constantly a benevolent influence in Helena's quest for her son's love, recalls the same conflict in her own youth:

> Even so it was with me when I was young.
>   If ever we are nature's, these are ours. This thorn
> Doth to our rose of youth rightly belong;
>   Our blood to us, this to our blood is born.
> It is the show and seal of nature's truth,
> Where love's strong passion is impressed in youth.[2]
>
> (I.iii.134-39)

The thorn and the rose, metaphors for sensuality and innocence, are terms used by the Countess to express the desired union between passion and purity. It is important to note here the similarity between the views of the Countess and Parolles. It is an ironic similarity, of course, for the Countess recognizes the value of both sensual passion and the pure innocence of youth, while Parolles rejects the virtue of chastity in favor wholly of what is "politic in the commonwealth of nature". Virginity for both the Countess and Parolles violates nature, but the "seal of nature's truth" for her includes purity as well as passion, while the "rule of nature" for Parolles sanctions unrestrained pleasures of the flesh and leads to the perversion of innocence by experience. The Countess' personal view of life and its relevance to the love quest of Helena associates both of these women with that rule or law of nature originating in the *lex aeterna*, which provides for a reconciliation between the demands of nature and the demands of spirit. Parolles' naturalistic sentiments, on the other hand, connect him with the libertine or demonic rule of nature. He represents those demands upon man which originate in the lowest level of the fallen world. In the course of the play his desire to "naturalize" Helena is thwarted and the aspect of nature which he symbolizes is "chastened".

---

[2]   *The Complete Plays and Poems of William Shakespeare,* ed. W. A. Neilson and C. J. Hill (Cambridge, Mass., 1942). All references to *All's Well* are from this edition.

Helena, at the point of selecting Bertram for her husband as a reward for curing the King of France of his fistula, comes more fully to realize the significance of the decision facing her, as well as its difficulty:

> The blushes in my checks thus whisper me,
> "We blush that thou shold'st choose; but, be refused,
> Let the white death sit on thy cheek forever,
> We'll ne'er come there again."
>
> Now, Dian, from thy altar do I fly,
> And to imperial Love, that god most high,
> Do my sighs stream.
>
> (II.iii.75-8, 81-3)

It is, in short, a matter of life or death. It brings shame to a young virgin to choose love, but it brings death (figuratively) for a maid not to choose to be a woman. Helena's initiation is a matter of flying from the altar of Diana to the altar of Eros. The two alternatives and their reconciliation are recognized by Helena earlier in the play:

> . . . if yourself,
> Whose aged honour cites a virtuous youth,
> Did ever in so true a flame of liking
> Wish chastely and love dearly, that your Dian
> Was both herself and Love, O, then give pity
> To her, whose state is such that cannot choose
> But lend and give where she is sure to lose.
>
> (I.iii.215-21)

The single identity of Diana and Eros, expressed in this speech to the Countess, identifies Helena's objective in the play. The accomplishment of this single identity not only solves Helena's personal problem and opens the way for the renewal of her life, it also stands as a metaphor for the harmonious union of the two warring levels of nature.

With the aid of divine forces manifest within her because of her chastity (which identifies her as an earthly counterpart of a heavenly virtue), Helena avoids the corrupt "naturalizing" influence of Parolles, and completes her initiation from maid to woman. The final stage of this journey into full feminine consciousness is reached with the help of the Florentine maid, Diana, an earthly counterpart of the goddess of chastity. Her seemingly more permanent virginity relates Diana to Helena in much the same way as Sabrina is related to the Lady in *Comus*. In both instances the virtue of the heroine is sustained and even heightened by an appeal to a figure of more refined or absolute virtue. The difference between Sabrina and Diana may be taken as a measure of the difference between Milton's and Shakespeare's mode of representation. Sabrina functions in *Comus* as a maid transformed into a goddess, while Diana functions in *All's Well* as a maid who bears a "significant association" with a goddess. In this role, Diana constantly assures her mother and Helena that she will not allow herself to be victimized by the "wanton siege" of Bertram. Diana's mother attests to her daughter's virtue in response to Helena's desire to know if Bertram solicits Diana:

> He does indeed:
> And brokes with all that can in such a suit
> Corrupt the tender honour of a maid.
> But she is arm'd for him and keeps her guard
> In honestest defence.
>
> (III.v.73-7)

Although Diana personifies the purity of chastity, she somewhat ironically enables Helena to consummate her marriage with Bertram. Through the substitution of herself for Diana, Helena is able to proceed in her initiation from what could be called a "virtual" marriage with Bertram to a true marriage. It appears, then, that through the character of the Florentine maid, Helena's earlier wish that the goddess Diana should be "both herself and love" is eminently fulfilled. The character of Diana serves as a chaste instrument (appearing unchaste) for achieving a virtuous sexual union (appearing sinful). As Helena herself remarks:

> Why then to-night
> Let us assay our plot; which if it speed,
> Is wicked meaning in a lawful deed
> And lawful meaning in a lawful act,
> Where both not sin, and yet a sinful fact.
>
> (III.vii.43-7)

To all appearances the assignation with Bertram is sinful; but in actuality it accomplishes a true marriage of Helena and Bertram, and fulfills Helena's desire that the law of chastity and the law of passion should be the same, or, in other terms, her desire to experience virtuously the transition from youthful virginity to womanly passion. For Helena, the entire experience indicates that

> ... the time will bring on summer,
> When briers shall have leaves as well as thorns,
> And be as sweet as sharp ...
>
> (IV.iv.31-3)

The thorns-leaves and sweet-sharp metaphors in this passage echo the Countess' metaphor of the rose and the thorn, which is in turn an expression of the natural or necessary correlation between Diana and Eros, purity and passion.[3]

The initiation of Bertram bears a close resemblance to that of Helena, for he also moves from a youthful condition to a mature condition and to the fulfillment of true love. His youthful condition, however, is one of ignorance and irresponsibility. Unlike Helena, he is unaware of the necessity for a change to take place in his life. For most of the action of the play he seems to be content in moving further away from those elements which will constitute his initiation into manhood. We are informed at the start of the play that Bertram is heir to the noble birthright of Rousillon, symbolized for him and for us by a ring given him by his father before he died, and which it is "the greatest obloquy i' th' world" to lose. "You must hold the credit of your father", he is told by Lafeu; but unfortunately his activities through most of the play indicate that he is unable to follow this advice. He is

---

[3] In *Genesis* (3.17-18), the addition of thorns to the rose is a curse of God, and thus a symbol for the fall of nature along with man. In Milton (*Paradise Lost*, IV.256), the image "without thorn the rose" is part of the Edenic vision, and thus a symbol of the pre-lapsarian condition of man and nature. The significance of this image in *All's Well* is that both the thorn of passion and the rose of innocence are included in Shakespeare's vision of a redeemed nature, the content of which is a harmony of both purity and passion. See G. W. Whiting, " 'And Without Thorn the Rose' ", *Review of English Studies*, X (1959), 60-2.

recognized by all as a young man who *appears* noble and honorable, but who as yet has given no proof that his heart is as noble as his physical bearing. The anticipation caused in the reader by this attitude toward Bertram is increased when the King of France reiterates in Paris the same sentiments heard at home:

> Youth, thou bearest thy father's face.
> Frank nature, rather curious than in haste,
> Hath well compos'd thee. Thy father's moral parts
> Mayst thou inherit too!

In the second act we discover that a number of young lords of the French court are leaving for the war in Florence, but Bertram is not allowed to go. He complains:

> I am commanded here, and kept a coil with
> "Too young" and "the next year" and "'tis too early".
>
> (II.i.27-8)

Parolles tempts Bertram to break this commandment and steal away to war with the other lords. In this temptation we can recognize the powerful influence Parolles has over Bertram, an influence instrumental not only in leading him away from love and into battle, but also in arranging the assignation with Diana. An excuse for breaking the King's commandment to remain absent from the war comes when Bertram is forced to marry Helena. Angered by this arbitrary act, he and Parolles leave for Florence. Ironically, the leading of Bertram by Parolles into a life of war and lustful love is demonic in its motivation, but the result is that Parolles, without of course intending to, leads Bertram away from an insular youthfulness into the experiences of life through which he comes eventually to reject Parolles and accept Helena. The irony of this circumstance repeats the ambiguous meaning in the play of Parolles' argument to "naturalize" Helena. In both instances Parolles means to corrupt (although he would not see it as corruption). In the first case, he ironically leads Bertram to a reconciliation with Helena. In the second case, Helena does come to be "naturalized", but on her own virtuous terms, rather than his corrupt terms.

The main stages of Bertram's initiation are his assignation-consummation with Diana-Helena, and his rejection of Parolles, experiences which occur in direct sequence in the play. The importance of Bertram's unwitting consummation of his marriage with Helena is emphasized by the double stipulation which, ironically, he himself imposes on Helena:

> When thou canst get the ring upon my finger which
> never shall come off, and show me a child begotten
> of thy body that I am father to, then call me husband . . .
> (III.ii.59-62)

The fulfillment of the second part of this sentence, accepted by Bertram at the end of the play, obviously constitutes the real marriage of the two characters, although Bertram at the time does not realize it. The ring, as already indicated, symbolizes the noble birthright handed down to Bertram by his father, but which he demonstrates through his actions he does not yet deserve. Nobility is not a simple matter of inheritance in the courtly world of this play, as the King of France explains in his well-known speech on the difference between an accident of noble birth and the performance of noble deeds. The deprivation of his ring by Helena (through Diana), then, symbolizes the temporary removal of Bertram's undeserved birthright. He must lose, so to speak, a nobility misunderstood by him to be a simple matter of inheritance before he can regain it by the performance of noble deeds. In addition, the ring serves as a traditional symbol for the marital union of Bertram and Helena. As the Countess remarks at the end of the play, "This is his wife; / That ring's a thousand proofs". At the end of the play Bertram emerges from the folly of his earlier life. In his rejection of Parolles and his acceptance of Helena he has earned in the proper way, through noble conduct, the right to the name of Rousillon.

While the action of initiation dramatizes the experiences of individuals, the pattern of purification in the play dramatizes both individual and civil experiences. The most important figure in this pattern of action is, again, Helena; she is responsible for the purification which takes place both on the individual and social level. She does not herself need to be purified (only initiated or reborn), for from the very start she possesses naturally a purity and healing power which relate her to the content of the divine world. Her qualifications as a purifier or redeemer are eminent, and are revealed to us in the play in a variety of ways. Shakespeare expresses her divinity, of course, in a manner more allusive and circumspect than that used by Spenser or Milton to indicate the same quality in Britomart and the Lady, for the conventions of the romantic mode of *All's Well* will not allow a certain limit of credibility to be exceeded. Helena does not have an enchanted spear, nor can she part a wall of flames; she is not attended by supernatural figures such as the Attendant Spirit or Sabrina. Although she is not surrounded by as much of the poetic marvelous as the other heroines, it is clear that Helena is a figure who represents the proper commerce between the world of spirit and the world of nature.

The first hint of Helena's unusual qualities comes in the form of the striking praise of her physician father spoken by the Countess. He was a man, she remarks, "whose skill was almost as great as his honesty; had it stretch'd so far, would have made nature immortal". We learn that Helena has inherited much of these virtues, and that her own personality contributes a power of goodness: "she derives her honesty and achieves her goodness". The first opportunity for Helena to employ these powers comes with her intention to travel to the court of France in order to cure the King of his fistula and to secure Bertram as a husband. Before she leaves she tells the Countess:

> You know my father left me some prescriptions
> Of rare and prov'd effects, such as his reading
> And manifest experience had collected
> For general sovereignty; and that he will'd me
> In heedfull'st reservation to bestow them,
> As cures whose faculties inclusive were
> More than they were in note.

(I.iii.227-33)

The Countess is not entirely convinced that Helena will be able to cure the invalid King, for "How shall they credit / A poor unlearned virgin, when the schools, / Emboll'd of their doctrine,

have left off / The danger to itself?" When Helena arrives in
Paris, the King has the same doubts:

> The congregated college have concluded
> That labouring art can never ransom Nature
> From her unaidable estate ...
>
> (II.i.12-4)

He believes himself past cure because of the failure of scientific
knowledge. Helena of course has other forces working for her:

> He that of the greatest works is finisher
> Oft does them by the weakest minister;
> So holy writ in babes hath judgement shown,
> When judges have been babes; great floods have flown
> From simple sources, and great seas have dried
> When miracles have by the greatest been denied.
> Oft expectation fails, and most oft there
> Where most it promises; and oft it hits
> Where hope is coldest and despair most fits.
>
> (II.ii.139-47)

This passage affirms the power of innocence. In addition, the
general contrast made between strong expectations and weak
hopes is meant, obviously, to be interpreted by the reader in
terms of Bertram's unfulfilled promise and Helena's unexpected
triumph.

Helena asks the King to trust the help of heaven through her
and not merely human skill. He begins to feel the power of the
young virgin:

> Methinks in thee some blessed spirit doth speak
> His powerful sound within an organ weak;
> And what impossibility would slay
> In common sense, sense saves another way.
>
> (II.i.178-81)

With the King's faith in her increasing, Helena makes a bargain
with him concerning the choice of husband; the cure is effected,
and the court rejoices in astonishment. Helena's first act of purification, the curing of the King, has effects beyond that of simple
medical health for one man. We have been led to believe, earlier
in the play, that the entire court has its share of corruptions,
symbolic of which is the sickness of the King himself. Parolles
remarks at one point that the lords of the court "move under

the influence of the most receiv'd star; and though the devil lead
the measure, such are to be followed". The court is under the
influence of a satanic music, a demonic counterpart to the divine
music of the spheres. The clown satirizes the shallowness of the
court in his sarcastic use of the phrase "O Lord, sir" as a suitable
courtly response to all questions and remarks. After Helena
restores him to health, the King is so revived that he delivers an
eloquent speech on the nature of an ideal society – in this case,
his court. In its emphasis on the necessity for noble actions instead of the dishonorable reliance on the accident of birth, the
King's speech has the dramatic effect of countering and obliter-
ating those satanic and irresponsible elements which had identified his court as a corrupt society. The inspiration for his speech
is, significantly, the noble and virtuous deed of the low born
Helena.

It is, ironically, Parolles who, together with the faithful old
lord, Lafeu, provides us with a characterization of Helena which
can leave no doubt about the divine influence she has over the
whole society of the play. Lafeu is the first to see that a trust in
empirical knowledge has its limitations: "They say miracles are
past; and we have our philosophical persons, to make modern
and familiar, things supernatural and causeless. Hence is it that
we make trifles of terrors, ensconcing ourselves into seeming
knowledge, when we should submit ourselves to an unknown
fear". He realizes that in Helena there is "A showing of a heavenly effect in an earthly actor". It is Parolles, however, who
makes the important conclusion:

> Par. Nay, 'tis strange, 'tis very strange, that is the brief and
> the tedious of it; and he's of a most facinerous spirit that
> will not acknowledge it to be the –
> Laf. Very hand of Heaven.
> Par. Ay, so I say.
> Laf. In a most weak –
> Par. And debile minister, great power, great transcendence;
> which should, indeed, give us further use to be made than
> alone the recov'ry of the King, as to be –
> Laf. Generally thankful.

(II.iii.33-43)

These last words, "generally thankful", may be read as a kind of epigraph for the thematic interests of the play as a whole. It is recognized that Helena's powers could and should be put to further use, and it is her total influence over the world of the play which resolves all conflicts in an atmosphere of general thankfulness. It is an expression suggesting the reintegration of the society, the return of wholeness and purity reflected in the ideal concept of nobility, the solution of Helena's love problem, the restoration of the prodigal Bertram, and the ultimate purgation of the demonic influence of Parolles.

The most important part of Bertram's purification occurs in the ritualized consummation of his marriage with Helena. It is Bertram himself who establishes the conditions of this true marriage in the letter concerning the ring and the child. The irony of this fact, plus the irony of the sexual substitution (Bertram believes he is seducing Diana, not fulfilling the conditions of the letter), indicate to the reader that Bertram was destined to be reconciled with Helena in a chaste love. In other words, the fulfillment of those conditions which were made to seem impossible, and the substitution of Helena for Diana are highly figurative ways of telling the reader that Bertram's fitting and proper place in life is to be married to Helena. His purification, or the purging of those forces which direct him away from Helena, is signified by removing an object of sinful desire (Diana) and replacing it with an object of virtuous desire (Helena). This occurrence is something the reader waits for and expects to happen.

Parolles is the final barrier between Bertram and his redemption; but the removal of this barrier is not a removal of Parolles himself from the society of the play. It is consistent with the nature of comedy, Frye suggests, that characters who serve to block the integration of the society or the union of the hero and the heroine are very often themselves integrated in a show of secure benevolence on the part of the society. Such characters are first reduced to ineffectuality and then admitted to the festivities of concord with which plays of this kind normally conclude. This is what happens to Parolles, with the additional element of his own personal purgation. Bertram is purged of

Parolles' influence, as is the society as a whole; Parolles himself is cleansed, and then admitted to the court celebration at the end of the play. The reduction or humiliation of Parolles, which strips him of his power and amounts to a purification, takes place through a series of incidents in which he is sent on a foolish mission to recover a lost drum, is captured by his own lords, and made to reveal his villainous and disloyal nature. A curious aspect of the main scene of Parolles' mortification is the consistent use of a number of terms suggesting the Christian purgation of sin. The information given by Parolles which reveals his disloyalty is referred to by one lord as a *confession*. Parolles at one point offers to take the *sacrament*. He pleads for his life and comments, "I would *repent* out the remainder of nature". And, finally, the rarity or monstrousness of his villainy is said to *redeem* him. All, without doubt, comically ludicrous allusions to a religious purgation. Shakespeare's parody of this process not only serves to mitigate the serious or dark overtones of the influence of Parolles in the play, but it also serves as a more earthly counterpart to the spiritual process, consistent with the technique throughout the play of making allusive rather than overt associations between the natural and the divine. Parolles, then, is reduced to ineffectuality as far as Bertram and the society are concerned; in addition, he vows to live in shame as a penance. At the end of the play Lafeu readmits Parolles to the court by saying to him, "though you are a fool and a knave, you shall eat".

The pattern of death and rebirth again involves both individuals and the whole society. It is, however, so fully displaced from the mythic mode of representation that it exists within the play in an even more circumspect or figurative way than the other patterns of action. It is, in fact, largely absorbed into these other actions. We cannot expect, of course, actual death and rebirth in a romantic comedy because of its proximity to the realities of normal human experience and the ordinary physical laws of nature. The figurative death in *All's Well* is even less directly indicated than in *Romeo and Juliet, Much Ado,* or *The Winter's Tale*. We learn that Helena deliberately has led Bertram to believe that she is dead in order that she may proceed more effectively with her scheme for winning him. Before selecting Bertram for her husband, Helena's cheeks blush with shame that a virgin must make such a choice; but if the choice is not made those cheeks will be forever white with death. The choice between love and perpetual virginity presents itself to Helena in terms of the alternatives of life and death. Virginity, in this play, is a condition which represents nature unfulfilled. The sensuality which is the opposite of virginity may take two forms. It may be a "naturalizing" sensuality in Parolles' sense of the word, in which case nature is corrupted rather than fulfilled. Or it may be a sensuality which is tempered by chastity, in which case the resulting condition of chaste love represents the desired fulfillment of nature. This is the condition Helena looks forward to, for it includes both the thorn and the rose; Diana and Eros become a single force. The virgin's trepidation in the face of this transformation from maid to woman is indicated in Helena's pretended death. The meaning of this pattern of action, however, is made evident almost entirely through the patterns of initiation and purification. The process of initiation for both Helena and Bertram is a dying to one kind of life and a rebirth into another. And the process of purification reawakens in Bertram and in a moribund society the desire for the renewal of virtue and true nobility.

We can at this point begin to see the central theme that emerges from Shakespeare's use of these patterns of action. The fictional world of *All's Well* is designed to reveal and ultimately to reconcile the diverse laws of nature. The technique is similar to that of Spenser and Milton; but, as I have already suggested, the identities of the demonic and the divine are more deeply hidden within nature in *All's Well* than they are in Books III and IV of *The Faerie Queene* and *Comus*. Shakespeare's concept of nature in this play is one in which the fallen world is pulled in the direction of the discord of corruption and in the direction of the concord of purity. This "tension of responsibility" for man is expressed through Bertram and Helena, who both find it necessary to establish some certain direction to their lives. Bertram, in the beginning, associates himself with the world of experience and wanton sensuality; Helena, at first, aligns herself with the world of innocence and virgin purity. It is his destiny to moderate sensuality with virtue; it is her destiny to accept the sensual without surrendering the virtue of chastity. The tension is resolved by the reconciliation of the lovers at the end of the play. It is a union which serves to represent the harmony of the diverse laws of nature, and their double demands upon man. The world (or the society) which prevails at the end of *All's Well* is an image of a redeemed or perfected nature. Its values, both social and personal, conform to the government of the universal law. The corruptions of nature (represented mainly by Parolles) have been removed; the conflict within Helena between the rose and the thorn has been resolved; the profligate Bertram has been restored to nobility; and the King and the court of France have been redeemed of their sickness.

In the initiation pattern of action, Parolles attempts to convince Helena of the rightness of his kind of "naturalization", but fails because of the value she attaches to her honor. This amounts to a defeat of the unregenerate level of nature; the victory is reinforced by Helena's success in transforming Bertram's sinful desires toward Diana into the consummation of their marriage. This raising of the level of nature in the direction of an order of virtue is accompanied by an acceptance rather than a rejection of the power of sensual passion. The resulting condition of nature corresponds precisely to Helena's desire to lose her virginity "to her own liking", to move from maidenhood to womanhood without sacrificing the conformity of her life to chastity. It also corresponds to the Countess' observation that both the thorn and the rose are "the show and seal of nature's truth".

In the pattern of purification, the theme of the redemption of nature is sustained on the social level by Helena's curing of the King. This restoration takes place only after natural science has exhausted its skill, and the divine power residing within Helena is employed. The King's return to health has the effect of restoring the whole court, or the whole society. This social or civil metaphor for the redemption of all nature is reinforced by the implied restoration of the court at Rousillon. Bertram, the new

Count of Rousillon, is transformed from prodigal to noble, enabling him to continue the virtuous tradition of his family and court. And, of course, the civil world could never have been cleansed without the removal of Parolles' influence. The theme is sustained on the more obscure level of the pattern of death and rebirth in the sense that a redemptive or perfected condition is represented by Helena's transcendence of the figurative white death, and her acceptance of a new life where Diana and Eros are one.

The King of France speaks from the perspective of sickness when he remarks that nature can never be ransomed from "her unaidable estate". Helena, whose chastity identifies her with the divine world of order, manages to do just that; she ransoms or redeems nature from its unaidable or fallen estate. The civil restorations and new lives with which *All's Well* concludes are metaphors which, taken together, imitate the ideal of a redeemed nature, a nature which is brought back into alignment with the *lex aeterna,* but which is not totally purged of the sensual forces of life. The condition of chaste love serves Shakespeare as well as Spenser as the prime image of this view of nature. It has such figurative possibilities in poetry because its establishment is the harmony in human life of the two disjoined laws of nature. The problem of bi-form man poised between the corrupt and the pure can be easily represented through the problem of love, in which the chaste heroine (in the three poems discussed here) is poised between wanton sensuality and perpetual virginity. The image of chaste love figuratively solves the problem of the chaste heroine by reconciling the pure with the passionate; it solves the problem of bi-form man by leading man away from the demonic and toward the divine; and, by extension, it solves the problem of a double nature by making diverse laws a single law.

It is, perhaps, fitting to conclude this study of the poetic imitation of a redeemed world with Shakespeare's play for more than one reason. The courtly world of *All's Well* represents the end of a significant progression from the world of fairy and the world of forest. A common interest in a redeemed world finds its expression in different ways in these three poems, each one of which is increasingly less "marvelous" in its poetic imitation, and increasingly more inclined to show the workings of the demonic and the divine within nature in a manner acceptable to a more realistic imagination. In addition, it is possible to observe that Shakespeare's poem is less "figural" than Spenser's or Milton's poem. The content of the divine world in *All's Well,* although still functioning in nature and quite important, is neglected in favor of a more frank and direct emphasis on the secular and fleshly nature of man. A more vital and human interest in the nature of man, in *All's Well,* replaces Spenser's elaborate emphasis on the more totally ideal condition of a divinely ordered nature, and replaces Milton's refinement of the natural world to a point where it hardly appears natural at all. Perhaps there is a significant relationship between the decline of the marvelous or the romantic mode of imitation, noticeable in these poems, and the rise of a more secular and temporal attempt to find a place in a universal order for the forces and drives of life.

CONCLUSION

The ideal expressed in the *Arcadia* may be taken as a compact statement of the synthesis which is the objective of each of the poems examined in the previous chapters: "Let beauty both, and chasteness fully reign." If we heed Miss Rosemond Tuve's recommendation that the reading of Renaissance poetry "on the figurative level has to be sustained rather than intermittent", it is not difficult to see that beauty and chasteness are "figures" for the two poles of the great antithesis of the age, and that their mutual sovereignty is a poetic image for the synthesis of nature and spirit.

The new valuation of nature which characterizes the consuming issue of the age is given expression in these poems through the romance world of beauty and love. A universal order of ethical force, however, is still required to temper the dangers inherent in the individual freedoms of the new naturalism. Chastity reigns together with beauty and love. This goal of world order has been referred to as "nature redeemed", a due proportion, a decorous relationship between nature and spirit. And it has been contended that this interest in cosmic harmony appears (in one of its disguises) in poetry as the dramatic resolution of the strife between the sensual and the pure. Each of the poems presents sexual desire as an image of the evil, chaotic, and corrupt aspects of nature; and virginal purity as an image of that aspect of nature most securely in touch with the divine order. The resolution of the strife is accomplished in terms of "chaste love", a characteristic Renaissance symbolic unity of two modes of being. It is the best of both possible worlds.

In the elaborate figurative use made of the drama of Venus and Diana, with its completion in the great image of chaste love, we can discern in these poems a thematic and formal expression of Renaissance concepts of reality. Thematically, the poems translate into dramatic action that traditional philosophy of history which has as its central condition the regeneration of the world, but with the important modification that the process of transformation must not wholly deny what is already there. In Renaissance poetics, informal as it is, we find the same vocabulary, involving the same condition and the same modification. The brazen or historical world is perfected by the golden or poetical world, but that very magical mirror (such as the one into which Britomart gazes) is held up to nature, not spirit. The three poems maintain limited analogical relationships between the natural and the supernatural in order to express immanence rather than transcendence.

This correspondence between poetic aim and formal elements is perhaps the most suggestive quality of these poems, which have been examined in relative isolation but may be taken, possibly, as exemplars of Renaissance poetic means and aims. The raising of a dramatic event (the mutual reign of beauty and chasteness) in these poems to the condition of a paradigm of cosmic order is in effect the transformation of a conceit into a microcosm. The little world of the poem, in its arrangement of images of beauty and purity, imitates the harmonious equilibrium of nature and spirit. The order of art recapitulates the order of the universe.

BIBLIOGRAPHY
(of works cited or consulted)

Abrams, M. H., *The Mirror and the Lamp* (New York, Norton Library, 1958).

Adams, John F., *"All's Well That Ends Well:* The Paradox of Procreation", *Shakespeare Quarterly,* XII (1961), 261-70.

Adams, R. M., *Ikon: John Milton and the Modern Critics* (Ithaca, 1955).

Alain de Lille, *The Complaint of Nature,* trans. D. M. Moffat, *Yale Studies in English,* XXXVI (1908).

Allen, D. C., *The Harmonious Vision* (Baltimore, 1951).

——, "Milton's *Comus* as a Failure in Artistic Compromise", *ELH,* XVI (1949), 104-19.

Arthos, John, *On a Mask Presented at Ludlow Castle* (University of Michigan Press, 1954).

——, *On the Poetry of Spenser and the Form of the Romances* (London, 1956).

——, "The Realms of Being in the Epilogue of *Comus",* *Modern Language Notes,* LXXVI (1961), 321-34.

Atkins, J. W. H., *English Literary Criticism: The Renascence* (London, 1951).

Auerbach, Erich, *Mimesis* (New York, Anchor Books, 1957).

——, "Figura", in *Scenes from the Drama of European Literature* (New York, Meridian Books, 1959).

Bacon, Sir Francis, *Essays, Advancement of Learning, New Atlantis, and Other Pieces,* ed. R. F. Jones (New York, Odyssey Press, 1937).

Baker, Herschel, *The Wars of Truth* (Cambridge, Mass., 1952).

Battenhouse, Roy W., *Marlowe's Tamburlaine* (Nashville, 1941).

Benesch, Otto, *The Art of the Renaissance in Northern Europe* (Cambridge, Mass., 1947).

Bennett, Josephine Waters, "Spenser's Venus and the Goddess Nature of the *Cantos of Mutabilitie",* *Studies in Philology,* XXX (1933), 160-92.

——, "Spenser's Garden of Adonis", *PMLA,* XLVII (1933), 46-80.

——, *The Evolution of The Faerie Queene* (Chicago, 1942).

Berger, Harry, Jr., "Spenser's Garden of Adonis: Force and Form in the Renaissance Imagination", *University of Toronto Quarterly,* XXX (1962), 128-49.

Bethell, S. L., *The Cultural Revolution of the Seventeenth Century* (London, 1951).

Boethius, *The Consolation of Philosophy* (New York, The Modern Library, 1943).

Bouwsma, William J., *Concordia Mundi: The Career and Thought of Guillaume Postel* (Cambridge, Mass., 1957).

——, *The Interpretation of Renaissance Humanism* (= Publ. No. 18, Service Center for Teachers of History) (Washington, D. C., 1959).

Bradner, Leicester, *Edmund Spenser and The Faerie Queene* (Chicago, 1948).

Bredvold, Louis I., "The Naturalism of Donne in Relation to Some Renaissance Traditions", *Journal of English and Germanic Philology*, XXII (1923), 471-502.

——, "The Religious Thought of Donne in Relation to Medieval and Later Traditions", in *Studies in Shakespeare, Milton, and Donne* (New York, 1925).

Brooks, Cleanth, "Milton and Critical Re-estimates", *PMLA*, LXVI (1951), 1045-54.

——, and John Edward Hardy, *Poems of Mr. John Milton* (New York, 1951).

Browne, Sir Thomas, *The Religio Medici and Other Writings* (London, Everyman's Library, 1951).

Bruser, Fredelle, "*Comus* and the Rose Song", *Studies in Philology*, XLIV (1947), 625-44.

Burke, Kenneth, "Symbolic Action in a Poem by Keats", in *Essays in Modern Literary Criticism*, ed. Ray B. West, Jr. New York, 1952.

——, "Criticism for the Next Phase", *Accent*, VIII (1948), 125-27.

Bush, Geoffrey, *Shakespeare and the Natural Condition* (Cambridge, Mass., 1956).

Calderwood, James L., "The Mingled Yarn of *All's Well*", *Journal of English and Germanic Philology*, LXII (1963), 61-76.

Campbell, Joseph, *The Hero with a Thousand Faces* (New York, 1949).

Carew, Thomas, *Poems*, ed. Rhodes Dunlap (Oxford, 1949).

Cassirer, Ernst, "Giovanni Pico della Mirandola", *Journal of the History of Ideas*, III (1942), 123-44; 319-46.

——, *The Platonic Renaissance in England* (Austin, Texas, 1953).

——, *The Myth of the State* (New York, Anchor Books, 1955).

Castiglione, Count Baldesar, *The Book of the Courtier*, trans. L. E. Opdyke (New York, 1929).

Cavendish, Richard, *The Image of Nature and Grace* (London, 1571).

Chapman, George, *Poems*, ed. Phyllis Brooks Bartlett (New York, 1941).

Chew, Samuel C., *The Virtues Reconciled* (Toronto, 1947).

Collins, Joseph B., *Christian Mysticism in the Elizabethan Age* (Baltimore, 1940).

Conger, G. P., *Theories of Macrocosms and Microcosms* (New York, 1922).

Curtius, E. R., *European Literature and the Latin Middle Ages*, trans. Willard R. Trask (New York, 1953).

Danby, John F., *Shakespeare's Doctrine of Nature* (London, 1949).

Dante, *The Divine Comedy*, Temple Classics (London, 1899-1901).

Davies, Sir John, *Works,* ed. A. B. Grosart, 2 vols. (Edinburgh, 1878).
Davis, Walter R., "Thematic Unity in the New Arcadia", *Studies in Philology,* LVII (1960), 123-43.
Dawson, Christopher, *Progress and Religion* (London, 1933).
Dickey, Franklin M., *Not Wisely But Too Well* (San Marino, Calif., 1957).
Du Bartas, Guillaume, *Divine Weeks,* trans. Joshuah Sylvester (London, 1621).
Durr, Robert Allen, "Spenser's Calender of Christian Time", *ELH,* XXIV (1958), 269-95.
Dyson, A. E., "The Interpretation of Comus", *Essays and Studies,* n.s. VIII (1955), 89-114.
Eliade, Mircea, *Birth and Rebirth* (New York, 1958).
Eranos Yearbooks, Papers from the, Vol. 2, *Spirit and Nature* (London, 1955).
Fairbanks, Arthur, *The Mythology of Greece and Rome* (New York, 1908).
Ferguson, Wallace K., *The Renaissance in Historical Thought* (Cambridge, Mass., 1948).
Ficino, Marsilio, *Commentary on Plato's Symposium,* trans. Sears Reynolds Jayne (= *University of Missouri Studies,* XIX) (1944).
Fletcher, J. B., *The Religion of Beauty in Women* (New York, 1911).
——, "A Study in Renaissance Mysticism: Spenser's 'Fowre Hymns' ", *PMLA,* XXVI (1911), 452-75.
——, *Literature of the Italian Renaissance* (New York, 1934).
Frye, Northrop, *Anatomy of Criticism* (Princeton, 1957).
——, "New Directions from Old", in *Myth and Mythmaking,* ed. Henry A. Murray (New York, 1960).
——, "The Structure of Imagery in *The Faerie Queene*", *University of Toronto Quarterly,* XXX (1962), 109-27.
Gello, John Baptista, *Circes of John Baptista Gello,* trans. Henry Iden (London, 1557).
Gilbert, Allan H., *Literary Criticism: Plato to Dryden* (New York, 1940).
Gilson, Etienne, *The Spirit of Medieval Philosophy* (London, 1936).
Greenberg, Sidney, *The Infinite in Giordano Bruno* (New York, 1950).
Greenlaw, Edwin, "The Captivity Episode in Sidney's *Arcadia*", in *Manly Anniversary Papers* (Chicago, 1923).
Greville, Fulke, *Poems and Dramas,* ed. Geoffrey Bullough (Edinburgh, 1939).
Grierson, H. J. C., *Cross-Currents in 17th Century English Literature* (London, 1929).
Guth, Hans P., "Allegorical Implications of Artifice in Spenser's *Faerie Queene*", *PMLA,* LXXVI (1961), 474-79.
Halio, Jay L., "*All's Well That Ends Well*", *Shakespeare Quarterly,* XV (1964), 33-43.
Hamilton, A. C., "Spenser's Treatment of Myth", *ELH,* XXVI (1959), 335-54.
——, *The Structure of Allegory in The Faerie Queene* (Oxford, 1961).
Hanford, J. H., *A Milton Handbook* (New York, 1946).
Haydn, Hiram, *The Counter-Renaissance* (New York, 1950).

Hebel, J. William, and Hoyt, H. Hudson, eds., *Poetry of the English Renaissance* (New York, 1938).

Hooker, Richard, *Of The Laws of Ecclesiastical Polity*, 2 vols. (London, Everyman's Library, 1907).

Hugh of St. Victor, *On the Sacraments of the Christian Faith*, trans. Roy J. Deferrari (Cambridge, Mass., 1951).

Hughes, Merritt Y., "Spenser's Acrasia and the Circe of the Renaissance", *Journal of the History of Ideas*, IV (1943), 381-99.

Huizinga, Johan, *The Waning of the Middle Ages* (London, 1924).

——, *Men and Ideas* (New York, Meridian Books, 1959).

Huntley, Frank L., "Sir Thomas Browne and the Metaphor of the Circle", *Journal of the History of Ideas*, XIV (1953), 353-64.

Jones, H. S. V., *A Spenser Handbook* (New York, 1930).

Jones, Leah, *The Divine Science* (New York, 1940).

King, Walter N., "Shakespeare's 'Mingled Yarn' ", *Modern Language Quarterly*, XXI (1960), 33-44.

Knowlton, E. C., "The Goddess Nature in Early Periods", *Journal of English and Germanic Philology*, XIX (1920), 224-53.

Kocher, Paul H., *Science and Religion in Elizabethan England* (San Marino, Calif., 1953).

Kristeller, Paul Oskar, *The Philosophy of Marsilio Ficino* (New York, 1943).

——, *Studies in Renaissance Thought and Letters* (Rome, 1956).

LaGuardia, Eric, "Chastity, Regeneration, and World Order in *All's Well That Ends Well*", in *Myth and Symbol*, ed. Bernice Slote (Lincoln, University of Nebraska Press, 1963).

Lawrence, W. W., *Shakespeare's Problem Comedies* (New York, 1931).

Le Comte, Edward S., "New Light on the 'Haemony' Passage in *Comus*", *Philological Quarterly*, XXI (1942), 283-98.

Lemmi, Charles W., *The Classical Deities in Bacon* (Baltimore, 1933).

——, "Britomart: the Embodiment of True Love", *Studies in Philology*, XXXI (1934), 133-39.

Lever, J. W., *The Elizabethan Love Sonnet* (London, 1956).

Levin, Harry, *The Overreacher: A Study of Christopher Marlowe* (Cambridge, Mass., 1952).

Lewis, C. S., "A Note on *Comus*", *Review of English Studies*, VIII (1932), 170-76.

——, *The Allegory of Love* (London, 1948).

——, *English Literature in the Sixteenth Century* (London, 1954).

Lipsius, Justus, *Two Bookes of Constancie*, ed. Rudolf Kirk (New Brunswick, N. J., 1939).

Lotspeich, Henry G., *Classical Mythology in the Poetry of Edmund Spenser* (Princeton, 1932).

Lovejoy, A. O., " 'Nature' as Aesthetic Norm", *Modern Language Notes*, XLII (1927), 444-50.

——, *The Great Chain of Being* (Cambridge, Mass., 1936).

——, and George Boas, *Primitivism and Related Ideas in Antiquity*, Vol. I of *A Documentary History of Primitivism and Related Ideas* (Baltimore, 1935).

Macklem, Michael, "Love, Nature and Grace in Milton", *Queen's Quarterly*, LVI (1949-50), 534-47.

MacLure, Millar, "Nature and Art in *The Faerie Queene*", *ELH*, XXVIII (1961), 1-20.

Mahood, M. M., *Poetry and Humanism* (New Haven, 1950).

Malraux, André, *The Metamorphosis of the Gods* (New York, 1960).

Mason, H. A., *Humanism and Poetry in the Early Tudor Period* (London, 1959).

Maxwell, J. C., "The Pseudo-Problem of *Comus*", *Cambridge Journal*, I (1948), 376-80.

Mazzeo, Joseph A., "Universal Analogy and the Culture of the Renaissance", *Journal of the History of Ideas*, XV (1954), 299-304.

McKeon, Richard, "Literary Criticism and the Concept of Imitation in Antiquity", in *Critics and Criticism*, ed. R. S. Crane et al. (Chicago, 1952).

Miller, Milton, "Nature in the *Faerie Queene*", *ELH*, XVIII (1951), 191-200.

Milton, John, *The Student's Milton*, ed. Frank Allen Patterson (New York, 1933).

Mueller, William R., ed., *That Soveraine Light* (Baltimore, 1952).

Munz, Peter, *The Place of Hooker in the History of Thought* (London, 1952).

Nelson, William, *The Poetry of Edmund Spenser* (New York, 1963).

Nicolson, Marjorie Hope, *The Breaking of the Circle* (Evanston, Ill., 1950).

Norton, Dan S., "The Tradition of Prothalamia", in *English Studies in Honor of James Southall Wilson* (Charlottesville, N. C., 1951).

Origen, *The Song of Songs: Commentary and Homilies*, trans. R. P. Lawson (= *Ancient Christian Writers*, No. 26) (1957).

Ovid, *The Metamorphoses*, trans. Horace Gregory (New York, The New American Library, 1960).

Padelford, F. M., "Spenser's Fowre Hymns", *Journal of English and Germanic Philology*, XIII (1914), 418-33.

——, "The Allegory of Chastity in *The Faerie Queene*", *Studies in Philology*, XXI (1924), 367-81.

Panofsky, Erwin, *Studies in Iconology* (New York, 1939).

Parkes, H. B., "Nature's Diverse Laws: The Double Vision of the Elizabethans", *Sewanee Review*, LVIII (1950), 402-18.

Pearson, Lu Emily, *Elizabethan Love Conventions* (Berkeley, 1933).

Pico, Giovanni, *A Platonick Discourse on Love*, ed. Edmund G. Gardner (Boston, 1914).

——, "Of the Dignity of Man", trans. Elizabeth L. Forbes, *Journal of the History of Ideas*, III (1942), 347-54.

Potts, A. F., *Shakespeare and The Faerie Queene* (Ithaca, 1958).

The First and Second Prayer-Books of King Edward the Sixth (London, Everyman's Library, 1910).

Randall, John Herman, *The Making of the Modern Mind* (Cambridge, Mass., 1940).

Raven, Charles E., *Natural Religion and Christian Theology* (Cambridge, 1953).

176 BIBLIOGRAPHY

Roche, Thomas P., "The Challenge to Chastity: Britomart at the House of Busirane", *PMLA*, LXXVI (1961), 340-44.
——, *The Kindly Flame*. A Study of the Third and Fourth Books of Spenser's *Faerie Queene* (Princeton, 1964).
Ross, Malcom M., *Poetry and Dogma* (New Brunswick, N. J., 1954).
Sandys, George, *Ovid's Metamorphosis Englished and Mythologized* (Oxford, 1632).
The Sarum Missal, trans. Frederick E. Warren, 2 vols. (London, 1911).
Saunders, Jason L., *Justus Lipsius: The Philosophy of Renaissance Stoicism* (New York, 1955).
Shakespeare, William, *All's Well That Ends Well,* ed. G. K. Hunter (London, 1959).
——, *The Complete Plays and Poems,* eds. W. A. Neilson and C. J. Hill (Cambridge, Mass., 1942).
Sidney, Sir Phillip, *The Countess of Pembroke's Arcadia,* ed. Ernest A. Baker (London, 1907).
Silverstein, Theodore, "The Fabulous Cosmogony of Bernardus Silvestris", *Modern Philology*, XLVI (1948-9), 92-116.
Smith, Charles G., "Spenser's Theory of Friendship", *PMLA*, XLIX (1934), 490-500.
Smith, G. Gregory, ed., *Elizabethan Critical Essays,* 2 vols. (London, 1904).
Speaight, Robert, *Nature in Shakespearian Tragedy* (London, 1955).
Spencer, Theodore, *Shakespeare and the Nature of Man* (New York, 1942).
Spenser, Edmund, *The Poetical Works,* eds. J. C. Smith and E. de Selincourt (London, 1912).
——, *The Works of Edmund Spenser,* ed. Edwin Greenlaw, et al., 9 vols. (Baltimore, 1932-49).
——, *Epithalamion,* ed. Cortlandt Van Winkle (New York, 1926).
Spingarn, Joel E., ed., *Critical Essays of the Seventeenth Century,* 3 vols. (Oxford, 1908).
——, *A History of Literary Criticism in the Renaissance* (New York, 1899).
Spitzer, Leo, "Classical and Christian Ideas of World Harmony", *Traditio,* II (1944), 409-64; III (1945), 307-64.
Stevenson, David L., *The Love-Game Comedy* (New York, 1946).
Stirling, Brents, "The Philosophy of Spenser's 'Garden of Adonis'" *PMLA,* XLIX (1934), 501-38.
Syford, Constance Miriam, "The Direct Source of the Pamela-Cecropia Episode in the *Arcadia*", *PMLA,* XLIX (1934), 472-89.
Tayler, Edward William, *Nature and Art in Renaissance Literature* (New York and London, 1964).
Taylor, Henry Osborn, *Thought and Expression in the Sixteenth Century,* 2 vols. (New York, 1920).
——, *The Mediaeval Mind,* 2 vols. (London, 1938).
Taylor, Jeremy, *Holy Living and Dying* (London, 1850).
Thompson, Guy A., *Elizabethan Criticism of Poetry* (Menasha, Wis., 1914).
Tillyard, E. M. W., *The Elizabethan World Picture* (New York, 1944).

Tillyard, E. M. W., *Shakespeare's Problem Plays* (Toronto, 1949).
——, *Milton* (London, 1951).
——, *The English Renaissance: Fact or Fiction?* (Baltimore, 1952).
Toffanin, Giuseppe, *History of Humanism* (New York, 1954).
Tuve, Rosemond, *Elizabethan and Metaphysical Imagery* (Chicago, 1947).
——, *Images and Themes in Five Poems by Milton* (Cambridge, Mass., 1957).
Watkins, W. B. C., *Shakespeare and Spenser* (Princeton, 1950).
Weinberg, Bernard, "Poetic Theories of Minturno", in *Studies in Honor of F. W. Shipley* (St. Louis, 1942).
——, "Scaliger versus Aristotle on Poetics", *Modern Philology*, XXXIX (1942), 337-60.
——, "Castelvetro's Theory of Poetics", in *Critics and Criticism*, ed. R. S. Crane, et al. (Chicago, 1952).
——, "Robortello on the Poetics", in *Critics and Criticism,* ed. R. S. Crane, et al. (Chicago, 1952).
Weston, Jessie L., *From Ritual to Romance* (New York, Anchor Books, 1957).
Whitaker, Virgil K., "Philosophy and Romance in Shakespeare's 'Problem' Comedies", in *The Seventeenth Century,* ed. R. F. Jones (Stanford, 1951).
Whiting, G. W., " 'And Without Thorn the Rose' ", *Review of English Studies,* X (1959), 60-62.
——, *Milton and This Pendent World* (Austin, Texas, 1958).
Whitman, C. H., *A Subject-Index to the Poems of Edmund Spenser* (New Haven, 1919).
Whitney, Lois, "Concerning Nature in *The Countesse of Pembrokes Arcadia*", *Studies in Philology,* XXIV (1927), 207-22.
Willey, Basil, *The Seventeenth Century Background* (London, 1934).
Williams, Kathleen, "Venus and Diana: Some Uses of Myth in *The Faerie Queene*", *ELH,* XXVIII (1961), 101-20.
Wilson, Harold S., "Some Meanings of 'Nature' in Renaissance Literary Theory", *Journal of the History of Ideas,* II (1941), 430-48.
——, "Dramatic Emphasis in *All's Well That Ends Well*", *Huntington Library Quarterly,* XIII (1950), 217-40.
Wimsatt, William K., and Cleanth Brooks, *Literary Criticism: A Short History* (New York, 1957).
Windelband, Wilhelm, *A History of Philosophy* (New York, 1935).
Woodhouse, A. S. P., "The Argument of Milton's *Comus*", *University of Toronto Quarterly,* XI (1941), 46-71.
——, "Nature and Grace in *The Faerie Queene*", *ELH,* XVI (1949), 194-228.
——, "*Comus* Once More", *University of Toronto Quarterly,* XIX (1950), 218-23.
——, "The Historical Criticism of Milton", *PMLA,* LXVI (1951), 1033-44.
——, ed., *Puritanism and Liberty* (Chicago, 1951).

INDEX

Abrams, M. H., 70-71
Adonis, 110-111, 117, 122, 145, 149
Alain de Lille, 24n, 27-29
allegorical interpretation, 58n
Ames, William, 14n
Aquinas, Thomas, 24n, 54-55
Auerbach, Erich, 11, 56-63, 75, 80
Augustine, Saint, 24n, 54-55

Bacon, Francis, 23-25, 66-67, 68, 72-73, 108
Baker, Herschel, 19n, 53
beauty, 43-44, 88-91, 169, 170
Bennett, J. W., 116n
bi-form man, 23, 27, 40, 133
Boas, George, 18n
Boccaccio, 58, 61-63
Boethius, 50
Bouwsma, William J., 88n, 93n
Bredvold, Louis I., 19n
Browne, Thomas, 26n
Bruser, Fredelle, 50n
Burke, Kenneth, 48n
Bush, Geoffrey, 19n

Carew, Thomas, 34-35
carpe diem, 44, 46-51
Cassirer, Ernst, 54, 55n, 108
Cavendish, Richard, 16
Chapman, George, 27
chastity, 39, 43, 83, 100-103, 104, 105, 112, 127, 137-138, 139-144, 146-147, 149, 150, 152-157, 166, 167, 169, 170; see also purity

compositum mixtum, 22-30, 51, 82
conceit, 170
concordia mundi, 72, 84, 88, 89, 91, 92, 94, 98, 100-101, 103, 109, 120, 122, 146
contemptu mundi, 47
Counter-Renaissance, 17-19
Curtius, E. R., 24n, 29

Danby, John F., 19n
Daniel, Samuel, 48-49
Dante, 25n, 58, 59-61, 80
Davies, John, 27, 32-34
Davis, Walter R., 40n
Dawson, Christopher, 25n, 54n
decorum, 11, 64, 71-75
Diana, 10, 31-51 passim, 82-83, 120, 154, 155-157, 163, 170
Du Bartas, Guillaume, 21-22, 26-27
Durr, Robert Allen, 87n

Eliade, Mircea, 152

Ferguson, Wallace K., 53n
Ficino, Marsilio, 89-91
fictional world, 10, 63, 64, 72, 75, 78, 83, 90, 99
figuralism, 11, 56-63, 72, 75, 80, 102, 122, 168
Forbes, Elizabeth L., 20n
form, 8, 64, 170; and substance, 121
Frye, Northrop, 11, 25n, 76-81, 102, 130, 148, 163

STUDIES IN ENGLISH LITERATURE

Out:

MOUTON & CO. — PUBLISHERS — THE HAGUE